Telling our stories
in ways that make us stronger

by Barbara Wingard and Jane Lester

Dulwich Centre Publications
ADELAIDE SOUTH AUSTRLIA

ISBN 0 9577929 2 1

Copyright © 2001 by
Dulwich Centre Publications
Hutt St PO Box 7192
Adelaide SA 5000, Australia
ph: (61-8) 223 3966 fax: (61-8) 8232 4441
email: dcp@senet.com.au
www.dulwichcentre.com.au

Typeset & Layout - Scott Nichols
Cover Photography - Phil Martin

Printed & manufactured by Graphic Print Group, Richmond, South Australia

Contents

Contents continued

Part 2 - Working together
towards culturally appropriate services

Introduction

By Barbara Wingard

As Indigenous people of this country, our stories are precious. They have survived over generations. Our elderly have passed them on to us and we will continue to pass them onto our children. We have our own ways of telling and listening to stories which are important to us.

When we come into contact with mainstream health services, either as clients or workers, sometimes we find very different ways of talking about people's lives. We find a focus on aims and objectives, or on projects which involve easily measured outcomes. Often these ways of speaking about people's lives do not fit comfortably for us (nor for many other people).

The telling of stories however is something we can relate to. As Aboriginal people, we have always told stories about our lives, and we know how important it is for people to be connected to their own stories, the stories of their family, their people, their history. These stories are a source of pride. When people become disconnected from them, life can be much harder to live.

Quite often, in many different ways, people seem to be looking only for problems. Even when walking down the street you can hear people say, 'what's your problem?'. People say things like that all the time! To get away from conversations that are only about problems we can invite the telling of particular stories and we can offer reflections on the things that are being said.

We must make it possible for people to be able to tell their stories in ways that are right for them. With Aboriginal people this means thinking through what would be a comfortable place for the conversations. It might mean sitting out on the lawn. The conversation might not be called counselling, but instead just talking together under the trees. Sometimes the environment and the way that people sit together makes it more likely for people to be able to tell their stories.

We also need to take care with how we begin conversations. When an Aboriginal person meets another Aboriginal person we work out how we know each other through our relatives. I might not know your parents, but who were their parents? We constantly reflect and remember these people and join with each other through our relations.

This process all happens before we think about talking about our own lives. Having connected in this way, rather than then asking any particularly direct question, we might just say something like: 'So, how's life been treating you?'. And this gives the person an opportunity to share whatever sort of story they choose. It gives them a chance to find their own way in the conversation.

Our people understand the significance of our stories, and the importance of taking care to tell them in the right places, to the right people and in the appropriate ways. Once these stories begin to be told we can then listen for the moments of change, the times when people are moving their lives in positive directions.

This is true in each person's story, but it is also true in relation to Aboriginal health in general. Sometimes if you look at only one part of the big picture within Aboriginal health it can seem as if nothing has happened, but that is not true. So much has happened over the last twenty years. There have been many changes to individuals' lives, to communities and to the ways we are talking about health issues. If we are not creating ways of telling the stories of change then they can get lost. The stories of hope and stories of pride need to be noticed, need to be told.

Not long ago, I was at a conference with Aboriginal health workers and found myself thinking about all the stories that existed within the room. Everyone's stories are different. We need to tell our stories, to have them written down. Each and everyone of us has a story to tell, where we have come from, the ways in which we do things now, the journey we have taken to get to where we are. It seems a good time for us to be telling our stories, documenting them and sharing them. Who knows what we will come up with?

In this book we have gathered together a number of different stories – stories of our own lives and our family's lives, but also a range of stories about hopeful work that is happening in relation to Aboriginal health and well-being. We hope the stories in these pages inspire you to tell your own.

As Indigenous people of this country, our stories are precious. They have survived over generations. Our elderly have passed them on to us and we will continue to pass them to our children. As Indigenous Australians we're going to keep telling our stories in ways that make us stronger.

Part 1

Stories of life and work

1

Coming Home:

voices of the day

By

Jane Lester

My name is Jane Lester and I am a descendant of the Yankunytjatjara/Antakarinya People from Central Australia and the Ewen Family who settled at Encounter Bay in 1836.

There was a time in the history of this country when human existence was 'one' with the Land. Prior to 1788, it is generally understood that at least 600 dialects of Aboriginal people lived in Australia. These peoples' existence was maintained by a highly evolved system that was nourished by at least forty thousand years of sharing, learning and living in universal oneness with Family, Country and Spirit. Conflict and breach of law were dealt with swiftly and systematically for the benefit of all. This land was traversed by ceremonial song lines which maintained connectedness between people, land and spirit.

Then, as we all know, there came the time when this country was proclaimed by the British as theirs to behold and control. I want now to invite us to remember those years and, to do so, wish to share with you some excerpts from the book *The People In Between: The Pitjantjatjarra People of Ernabella*. This was written by Winifred Hilliard in 1968:

The European arrived, settled on land that took his fancy, fenced his block and ensured that his claims were set down in writing. He assumed that the native could go elsewhere, there was plenty room. The European was ignorant of, or ignored the fact that the native lived within prescribed boundaries, known and acknowledged, with which his Dreamtime and ceremonial life were intimately involved. No written agreements existed, but the country on which a man hunted was his in a special and spiritual way. He could not move over without trespassing upon the domain of another, nor without severing the spiritual ties which gave him reason for being. The general attitude of the Europeans in South Australia, as elsewhere, has shown a marked willingness to believe the worst of the native people. Where there was no evidence, the worst was assumed as being the only reasonable explanation of strange actions. Such traditions die hard and they can be traced through the years until within the last generation. The decline of native tribes of South Australia followed settlement in 1836, despite fifty years of experience in other colonies from which to learn. (p.31)

The stealing of land was backed up with the power of guns and the decline of Aboriginal clans was inevitable with the added onslaught of new diseases. Throughout the country Aboriginal People were seen as a problem to the growing colony and only a few dared to write contrarily. Edward John Eyre, the explorer, wrote in 1840:

The character of the Australian native has been constantly misrepresented and traduced, that by the world at large he is looked upon as the lowest and most degraded of the human species, and generally considered as ranking but little above the members of brute creation. It is said, indeed, that the Australian is an irreclaimable, unteachable being; that he is cruel, bloodthirsty, revengeful and treacherous; and in support of such assertions, references are made to the total failure of all missionary and scholastic efforts hitherto made on his behalf, and to the many deeds of violence or regression committed by him upon the settler ... I believe were Europeans placed under the same circumstances, equally wronged, and equally shut off from redress, they would not exhibit half the moderation or forbearance that these poor untutored children of impulse have invariably shown. (in Hilliard 1968, p.32)

Eyre went on to write:

> *It is often argued, that we (the settler) merely have taken what the natives did not require, or were making no use of ... It is true that they (the native) do not cultivate the ground; but have they, therefore no interest in its productions? – Does it not supply grass for the sustenance of the wild animals upon which in a great measure they are dependent for their subsistence? – does it not afford roots and vegetables to appease their hunger, water to satisfy their thirst, and wood to make their fire? – or are these necessaries left to them by the white man who comes to take possession of their soil? Alas, it is not so! All are in turn taken away from the original possessors ... All that they have is in succession taken away from them – their amusements, their enjoyments, their possessions, their freedom – and all that they receive in return is obloquy and contempt, and degradation and oppression.* (in Hilliard 1968, p.32)

These words were written 160 years ago. They foresaw much of what was to come. By the early 1900s Aboriginal protection policies and reserves had been established. Aboriginal people began living an imprisonment, in which every aspect of their lives was to change to the white way. They were supervised by superintendents known only as 'The Boss'. Everything had to be approved by him or his missus. Aboriginal lives were lived at the whim of these people. If a superintendent did not feel like driving anyone to the Doctor, they didn't. If the Aboriginal person subsequently died, then there was no recourse. Poverty was rife within Aboriginal communities, education was poor, job opportunities few, and racism unnamed and riding high.

The Churches and missionaries played a significant part in this story. What were believed to be 'pagan' ways were to be crushed, and what were believed to be the 'right' ways to live were to be imposed. Missions were established to house neglected and unfortunate children, in particular those of mixed blood, and contact and connection with Family and old ways were persistently discouraged.

By 1936, assimilation policies were being established and exemption cards were being introduced for Aboriginal People. This card allowed certain Aboriginal People to leave reserves and access broader employment opportunities. By applying for and being approved for exemption meant you were no longer allowed to frequent reserves or associate with Aboriginal People on reserves. By signing agreement to carrying these cards you were legally saying you were no longer Aboriginal.

Resistance

Throughout all of these years, Aboriginal people resisted every step along the way. They resisted the settlers' occupations of their homelands and when they were forcibly removed from their homes/their land they strove to maintain their own ways of living, their families and their links to country. In whatever form was available they retained their links to their home, and they sought justice, in every way possible.

Their continual efforts led in 1967 to a Federal Referendum on whether to include Aboriginal People as citizens of this country. It was successful and is still seen as a landmark in our history. In the 1970s their resistance led to a Royal Commission into Land Rights. In 1971 Senator Bonner was the first Aboriginal person to be elected to Parliament. 1974 saw the end of the White Australia policy. And in 1979 the Pitjantjatjarra Land Rights Bill saw land returned to Aboriginal people and a precedent was set for many Aboriginal peoples to be able to reconnect with their homelands.

In more recent history, throughout the 1980s, the Aboriginal struggle continued. In 1981 The World Council of Churches delegation released a report on the condition of Aboriginal People in Australia and as a result the Human Rights Commission was established. 1985 saw the commencement of a campaign to investigate the reasons for the high number of Aboriginal Deaths in Custody. The historical and ongoing links between the Police and Aboriginal oppression were finally being talked about. Deaths in custody is a phrase that every Australian is now familiar with.

In 1988 the Bicentenary of the arrival of the first fleet of Europeans to Australia saw Aboriginal People from all over the country travel in convoy, rallying in every major city. Their destination was to stand as one at Lady Macquarie's Chair, overlooking Sydney Harbour to protest and voice their disgust at the idea of celebrating the beginning of the demise of Aboriginal People and their culture. Many peoples stood together in solidarity, some of whom had never seen city streets before. It was a defining moment for Aboriginal Australia.

The last decade has seen tumultuous change. The Mabo and Wik High Court decisions which reaffirmed Aboriginal rights to land, and the rise and fall of the racist One Nation Party, have meant that Australia has been grappling on a daily basis with the relationship between Aboriginal and non-Aboriginal Australia.

The marches for reconciliation that have taken place throughout the country have offered a glimpse of a different future for this nation, as has the symbolism associated with the Sydney Olympics. Now, increasingly, Indigenous leaders are trying to harness this momentum to create a long sought after treaty.

Remaking connections

And all the while, Aboriginal Australia has continued to remake and build upon connections with home and our own ways of living. I now want to talk about how this has occurred in my own life and with my own family.

Four years ago Aboriginal people in Australia were invited to attend meetings in their regions with Commissioners from the Human Rights Commission regarding the removal of Aboriginal Children from their families. This invitation sent a surge through the community. Finally the world was about to hear about what really happened, why tens of thousands of Aboriginal children disappeared from their black mother's eyes, some never to be seen again.

My father was stolen. He was part of the Stolen Generation. His forty or so first cousins were also stolen. They made up one entire mission home. They weren't allowed to talk their language, they weren't allowed to eat bush tucker. They were removed a thousand miles from their country so that they couldn't be brought back home.

When the enquiry came to Adelaide we supported our older generation to give private interviews with regard to the impact of being taken away. The whole process was like trying to close the circle for my grandmother. She lost seven of her children, that's all the children she had. She lost each and every one in four different batches of abduction. The enquiry was a chance to be able to reconnect the circle and take the family back to her. Even though she's not living physically she's still there in spirit. We can be honouring of her by honouring the blood connection we have, and by being able to sit on the land that she walked. Going to the enquiry was an honouring of my grandmother.

As members of the younger generation we gave interviews too. With two of my first cousins, who in Aboriginal ways are my brother and sister, we requested to have a private interview. We wanted to share our experiences of how the Stolen Generation didn't just impact on the first generation. It impacted the second. It's impacting the third, and it will potentially go on if we can't find ways to resolve the loss and make reconnections. The three of us went to the enquiry together. I'm a non-drinker but I felt like I could have drunk a bottle of scotch or something before getting in there! We knew we would be talking about painful things.

In the private interview with my brother and sister, we talked of how there was love in our family and yet there wasn't a real love because there was so much fear – 'If you love your child, your child gets taken away'. We spoke of how when we were born we weren't citizens in this country. Welfare or the department, anyone, had the right to just walk in and take us away. Our parents didn't have the right to say no. They could say it but it wasn't heard. We spoke of the lack of parenting skills that we had, the loss of our language, the loss of our culture. We spoke of how our connectedness to our whole being and our relationships with our families were gone. Finding that one generation of your whole family made up a mission home for so many years is quite a hard thing to come to terms with.

When we talk about the enquiry now all these years down the track, my brother and sister and I always laugh about this one box of tissues. At one stage the three of us were sitting there having a good howl, and we'd used up all the tissues that we had brought. So Mick Dodson, the Commissioner, asked for one of his team to go and get a box of tissues. They went off quite discreetly and quietly. When they brought the tissues in, Mick took them and grabbed this great handful for himself. Then he sat the box on his knees. We didn't even get offered them! They were for him not for us! We found that quite humorous! He conducted the process in such a loving way, it was beautiful.

As the report went into parliament there were many eyes on television sets to see how it was going to be accepted. I watched with a lot of doubt, but I could actually feel that some of the politicians were saddened, that some did know that white Australia does have a connection to what happened to black Australia. Then we watched as all the different churches started to say that they were sorry for what they had done. Sorry is a very easy word to be shared, but at least it's a start. What we still need is access to records and a lot of the records that are tied up within the missions are not collated and therefore they're inaccessible. Sorry is a start but what we need now is action to help people come home.

Coming home

For the last ten years within our family, we've been very persistent with our older generation about the need for them to take us home – to teach us where we come from, to teach us who our family is, so that we can regain our identity. We've mainly focussed on our aunties. I come from a family that has a very high number of women. So we pleaded with our aunties to take us back. In 1993 they organised for us what we call the 'homecoming ceremonies'. Thirty of us travelled all together in a convoy out to Oodnadatta and then various relatives of ours, our grandmothers and mothers and sisters and children, travelled from various areas all to this one location. We were put through a range of rituals and ceremonies to let the ancestors know that we were back in our country, to let our families know that we still had a need to be connected to the family, and to signify that we recognised that we had a hell of a lot of learnings that we needed to rediscover.

We spent one week doing this process, and there were some really magical moments. Of course, when any magical moment occurs, there are always the hard moments that happen too. It was a very exciting adventure for me. Over the years of growing up I always knew I was Aboriginal and I had often travelled within South Australia and the Northern Territory. I knew I belonged somewhere along that line but never knew exactly where. It took me many years to find out exactly where I come from. It's only been in the last twelve years that I can say that I'm a Yankunytjatjara/Antakarinya woman. I was quite sad when I recognised that, as a child, I had actually been at times in my traditional area and didn't even know it. But when I found out where I came from I was actually standing there, on my country. When I was told, 'You're from here', it was an amazing moment.

Trying to find out where I was from was a long process. Starting the ball rolling was the hardest thing to do. Ironically it eventually got to a point when I didn't have to look any more - things began to fall in my lap. But all along the way it took courage. I remember when I was invited to go to a conference out in the Pitjantjatjarra lands. I went there and there was this old woman who sat in the conference for the two days. She was from the area, and there was a whole range of other black fellas from all over the state. For two days I looked at this woman and I knew I was connected to her but I felt it would be stupid to go up to her and say, 'Well, I don't know who you are but I reckon we're connected ...' Eventually when the two-day conference finished it came to a point that I knew I had to choose whether to say something or not. Finally, I went up to her and said 'I don't know why I'm saying this, but I believe that there's a connection between me and you', and she said, 'Well, who are you?'. And I said 'I'm Jane Lester, I'm Colin Lester's daughter'. And this woman just burst into tears and wrapped her arms around me. She's my dad's first cousin.

Once I started there were a range of stories like that. We have a joke that we have a sacred site at the petrol station toilets at Pt Wakefield! There were a hundred of us one time, this is years later, when we were all travelling up to Uluru. My eldest daughter was four at the time, and I was trying to get her into the toilet quick. I got her into the toilets and when we were coming out I could see this whole queue of Aboriginal women and kids. There was this woman in the queue and when I looked at her my heart did a somersault. It just sort of projected out of my body, and I thought, 'Oh, here we go again, I'm going to have to ask this question again'. So I walked up to her and I said, 'I don't know why I'm saying this, but, you know, I think there's something between you and me. My name's Jane Lester, I'm Colin Lester's daughter.' And, you know, the same thing happened, she burst into tears, and wrapped her arms around me. Another first cousin of my father. Gradually I didn't have to justify any more who I was, people knew who I was. I knew where I was from. I walked my own country. The people I feel most sadness for are those people who traditionally come from the land where there is now a city or a town because so much of their story has been stepped upon, different sites have actually been lost. That's where I am at a privilege. There are still parts of my country that have only been walked by people of my bloodline.

We must find ways for everyone to come home. Even if we can't reconnect with our immediate family we can still reconnect with our land, still reconnect to our extended family. We can find someone who knows the connections. We don't need a white system to do that. It's about trying not to hear the ripples and the words of the system and instead to follow the words and ripples of our heart, of our people. From time immemorial Aboriginal learning has been shared through stories, and because of this almost invariably it is possible to find someone who has a piece to your puzzle. Even if you've been adopted out and put in another country you can come back to this country and sit down with any people and say 'Do you have any idea where I come from?', and they'll point you in the direction. Whether they are drunk or whether they're sober they will be able to do it. Eventually if we keep on following the directions we're gonna find where we come from. And we don't need no piece of paper to tell us that's where we come from. The people will know, and we will know. And ever so gradually you find more connection.

Resurgence

Aboriginal culture is one of the oldest if not the oldest Indigenous culture in the world. It has survived for so long. It was fragmented in a very short space of time but people are now going back to where they come from. We are finding ways of addressing the cultural homelessness that has been imposed upon us. We must continue to find ways in which we can come home to our culture, to our land and families. Everyone will do this in a different way, to a different degree, but there is, I believe, a strong wave happening across the country. We are coming back home. We are reconnecting with our spirit places. Stories of homecoming are being told across the land. There is a resurgence happening and it will change this country.

Reference

Hilliard, W. 1968: *The People In Between: The Pitjantjatjarra People of Ernabella*. London: Hodder & Stroughton.

2

Stories of life

By

Barbara Wingard

Throughout our lives there are particular stories that are significant to us. These are stories that we carry with us and which make us who we are. In this chapter I am going to tell some of the stories that I carry with me into my work as an Aboriginal Health Worker. I hope that by telling these stories it might help you to think more about the stories of your own life and of your family and community and how these stories are precious.

Stories from school

When I was a child you had to be six years old in order to start school. I was a very tall and skinny six year old and I didn't fit in very well at Norwood Infants. Before I knew it I was sent up to the primary school and put in what was called the 'Opportunity Class'. This was a class full of different cultures. There were about four Aboriginal kids, some children with Italian background, and others who were Anglo-Australian. We were the slow learners, or the kids who had spent a lot of time in hospitals. We were the ones who were seen to be behind in our schooling.

We were all called 'dummies' for being in that room and I was also called 'blackie'. I found it awful being called these names but from the very beginning I knew that I was a lot luckier than some of these other children, and this knowledge was significant to me. I remember so clearly the most powerful thing that ever happened to me at school. At times, the teacher of the Opportunity Class would leave the room and I would be put in charge. I loved this. I can still feel the sense of pride that came from being asked to be responsible. It was very empowering for me. Being offered that small sense of responsibility was a key turning point in my young life. I can remember it so clearly. It offered me enough confidence to begin sticking up for some of the other kids – those who couldn't look after themselves. I would look after them and keep away the other children who would say hurtful things.

Finding pride and company in hard times

By the time I was thirteen I had learnt a lot of practical skills in that Opportunity Class – how to iron and sew. But it got to the point where I knew school was doing me no good. The age for leaving school at that time was fourteen, but if you found work you could leave earlier. At thirteen I got my first job at the Box Factory where most of the workers were Italian and Greek women. I had figured out that if I had nothing up there in my head, as I had been told for many years, then at least there was nothing wrong with my hands. Working on the machines in the factory was very fast work and I was very good at it. Learning that I could work well with my hands was a significant event in my life. It was another source of pride.

Despite this, I don't have a lot of good memories from around that time. My father died not long after I started at the Box Factory. He had a heart attack and passed on, a week off his fortieth birthday. So many of our people die so young. At about the same time, the factory went through a hard time and they put some of their workers off – including me.

I turned to house-keeping work and became a housemaid for a motel down in Adelaide. I also did ironing for other people whom I had met. Leaving school so early and working in those environments, I was very mature for my age. At times I felt like an old lady. I think what really helped during this time was going into various factories, meeting people of different cultures and listening to their stories.

I'll never forget the sad stories of the war. Within the factories in Adelaide there were women from Europe who had suffered so much during the Second World

War. I heard women share their stories of being raped and other events that they had survived. I recall one older Polish woman in particular who spoke to us about the bashings and the rapes. She found these stories hard to tell to us. They were very private stories and we all found them hard to hear. But something about the telling and the listening was significant to all of us. Her stories and those of the other women stayed with me. They are still with me. It was a powerful learning for me as a young woman to understand these stories. They made me reflect on my own life, in helpful ways. In Australia while I was growing up, there was a lot of racism and in many different forms. Hearing the stories of those European women, what they had survived and how, helped me in some way to deal with all that was happening around me. Those women also introduced me to a love of stories. As we grow up, we all listen to other people's stories of their journeys. I think listening to these stories makes us who we are.

Dealing with restrictions

At this time, we were living in Norwood, Adelaide and it was very difficult for Aboriginal people to rent homes. It was a time when there were still many restrictions as to when and how Aboriginal and non-Aboriginal could mix with each other. Some Aboriginal people were given exemptions under the Aborigines Act which allowed them to mix with the wider community. These exemptions were written on little cards which our people called 'dog tags'. These dog tags allowed Aboriginal people to move into white society. Aboriginal people with exemptions could drink in pubs and do all those sorts of things. My grandmother used to live at Point Pearce (an Aboriginal mission) but she received an exemption when she was sixteen which is why we were able to be living in Norwood in the 1950s and 1960s. I imagine she must have applied for this exemption seeking for something more out of life for her family than that which was available on the mission. Once an exemption was granted to one person it was automatically granted to other members of their family. My father was therefore automatically given one of those exemption cards.

But having an exemption did not mean an end to restrictions on your life. There were many restrictions on Aboriginal people mixing with one another. I can remember walking down Norwood Parade with an very old elderly uncle and getting booked by the Police. We got picked up by the Police and booked for consorting together. He was from the country and was absolutely devastated when the Police man got out his little book and wrote our names in it. Things like this were regular occurrences for Aboriginal people in those times.

The Exemptions basically indicated that you had the legal status of whites but this created a lot of problems amongst Aboriginal people. We had to try to overcome a sense of them and us. Those who were granted exemptions had to deal with accusations from other Aboriginal people. Statements like 'Those fellas think they are white' were commonplace. As time has gone by there is a now an acknowledgement that these divisions were created by government policy, and that each Aboriginal family was simply trying to find the best way to survive the racism and complexities of those times.

Working for life

I remember as a young girl feeling like we as a family had been thrown to the wolves. We had been granted an exemption and were therefore making our way in the white society, but it felt as if we were alone in a hostile world. We had a very strong identity of who we were and where we were from, but with all the racism that was around in those days it just didn't feel as if we belonged. As we had been granted exemptions we were not entitled to any Aboriginal monies or any Aboriginal 'benefits' for clothes or shoes. It required pretty hard work just to get by, so that is what we did. We worked.

I not only started working early, I also got married early – at sixteen. I was mixing with older people and did not have many young friends, other than my immediate family. When I got married I settled in a working class suburb called Elizabeth. I remained there for eight years after I separated from my husband but I really wanted to get my children away from that neighbourhood. There were not a lot of things for young children to do in that area. My brother was living in Murray Bridge, and so I decided to move up here. I have been here ever since and have never regretted it. It has been a great place for my children. There is a sense of freedom in places like this as it still a country area. It seems a lot safer somehow.

Before I left Adelaide I was working cleaning cars to earn a little extra money on top of my single mother's pension. When I told my employers that I would be moving they found me work at a related dealership in Murray Bridge. It was 1976. At the same time I saw an advertisement for the first Aboriginal health worker position for the Murray Bridge area. I looked at it and thought that I would have no chance as it was a government job, but I applied for it anyway. When I was successful, two people came out to the car dealership to tell me. They broke the news to me that I was successful at winning the job and I cried. I'll never forget that. I got really quite upset. Fancy me with a government job.

During the job interview one of the ladies had asked me lots of questions and I remember saying, 'There are a lot of things I don't know, but I am willing to learn'. She reckoned that really helped me a lot but I was just telling the truth. There were a lot of things I didn't know. I hadn't finished school. I was twenty-nine, with three children. They must have thought that it might be worth giving me a go. I have been with Aboriginal health for the last 24 years.

Starting work in Aboriginal health

I remember how scared I was on my first day of work. I didn't have any of the office skills that I was going to need. Answering the phone terrified me. Each time it would ring I would cough and sweat. We'd never had a phone. I had to learn everything from scratch. I was really lucky that a community health nurse from Adelaide was working with me. She came up for three days a week and worked by my side to teach me how to file and work in an office. I remember that a part of my job was to go to other government departments, introduce myself and get to meet people. This terrified me a great deal. My only experience of government departments, particularly before I got my pension, was going to the welfare to get money for my children and myself to live on. That had always been a begging situation. I always had to share a lot of my personal details about why my husband was no longer with me. They would ask a lot of personal questions and I always felt like I was crawling for the money. That was why I so wanted to get a job. I had spent eight years waiting for that pension cheque and that was enough. Waiting for a cheque every fortnight doesn't do anything for your confidence. I understand what it is like for other people on benefits.

I have always found being an Aboriginal Health Worker to be a wonderful job. It is about going into people's homes, visiting people, seeing how they are, listening to their stories in ways that are helpful, and making it possible for them to be able to utilise the services that are available for them. Although there have been many changes, people are still reluctant to use some mainstream services because of the past policies directed at Aboriginal people.

These of course are the policies of assimilation, such as the dog-tags I mentioned before, as well as policy of removing Aboriginal children from their families and homes. There have been so many policies directed at Aboriginal people by governments and health and welfare officials. They have made a big impact on people's lives and a big impact on how Aboriginal people view health and welfare services.

Our old people have many stories about government and welfare. I remember welfare used to come to our house and look in our ice box. They used to be able to come into people's houses and check people's sheets, and how much food was in their houses. And of course it was welfare who used to take the children away. These weren't uncommon practices and they have had a big influence on our feelings about government departments. When I first began working in a government department my hands were really clammy and sweaty. Everyday I walked into work I felt like I was walking into a police station. If I felt like this, and I was working there, then I could understand why other Aboriginal people were not using government services.

For us early Aboriginal health workers there were so many things that we had to find our way with. For me, in the beginning one of the hardest was eye contact. Where I come from we don't have a lot of direct eye contact. We don't eye ball each other all the time. You don't stare at each other in Aboriginal culture. If you do have eye contact it is usually quite quick, quite brief. It was really scary for us health workers to learn how to do eye contact with people. We had to, because in the white man's world if you don't look at somebody in the eye people assume that you are telling lies and are untrustworthy. I remember us as health workers all meeting together and saying we can't do this. But for those of us working in mainstream environments, it was a very good tool for us to learn. Now we can look people in the eye. Another good thing about the eye contact was that it offered us more confidence. When I am doing cultural awareness work I still talk about eye contact as a skill we have learnt because it does not come naturally to us. I never used to walk around looking at people in the eye. Now, though, I can eye ball people and it won't be me putting my head down - it will be them lowering their eyes! As early Aboriginal health workers we knew we had to learn these things, we knew if we learnt them it would be easier for those who would come after us.

Witnessing stories

As an Aboriginal health worker I soon learnt that it was my role to go to people's homes, to listen to their stories and to find ways of assisting them to maintain or improve their health. When I think about some of the people who I have worked with over the years I think about some of the older ones who aren't here anymore. I think of the stories that they used to tell of their survival skills – of how they would fish around here, camp around here, and the ways in which they would live off the land. When I used to visit these older people they liked to talk about the old days. I was a witness to these stories. I would hear the most wonderful things.

My role was to link people in the community with others and with services, and to listen and witness their stories. Some people don't listen to stories. They think, 'Oh, those times, they were the olden days'. I think every child goes through this with their parents. I remember saying that to my mum and I have heard my kids say it to me – ' Oh, here we go again.' But there is a time in life where this changes. All of a sudden people want to ask questions, about who they are and where they are from. When I would visit families, often there would be someone who clearly needed to tell particular stories. They needed someone to listen to them, and to encourage them to talk about some particular things. I would be their witness. It was a real honour that these elderly people wanted to share their stories with me.

Our family stories

When I listen to my mother's stories we sometimes think, we need to write this down, we need to document these things. My mum is 79 and doing very well as an Aboriginal person to make it that long. We know we are very lucky to have her. My daughter and I are thinking of taking my mum back to Bordertown where she grew up. When we are there we will ask her to tell her stories and then we will write them down. Everyone needs a witness to the stories of their life. In Bordertown the Aboriginal community has beautiful big houses which they made out of flattened kerosene tins. Back when my mother was living in Bordertown, these houses were on council land but this land has now been given back to the Aboriginal people. That is the place of my birth. The place of my birth has now been reclaimed as Aboriginal land. There is a lot we are still to reclaim but we can't say that nothing has changed. A great deal has changed in my lifetime.

3

Introducing 'Sugar'(Diabetes)

by

Barbara Wingard[1]

I'd like to tell the story of 'Sugar' because to me it is a story of trying to find new ways of working, of trying different things, taking new steps. In early 1996, as a member of the Aboriginal Women's Health and Healing Project[2], I had the opportunity to watch a video of the work of the CARE counsellors of Malawi.

This video showed the ways in which people in Malawi (a small country in south eastern Africa) were using externalising conversations in ways that were assisting them to join together in dealing with the hardship being caused by HIV/ AIDS[3].

The ten of us involved in the Aboriginal Women's Health and Healing Project really enjoyed watching this video. It really touched me very strongly and I couldn't wait to come home and work with the ideas. I specifically thought about how this sort of work could be used with diabetes as it is an illness that is causing a lot of harm within Aboriginal communities. Not long before watching the video, a doctor had asked us here at Murray Mallee Community Health Centre to organise something for three people who were very sick with diabetes and constantly coming into hospital.

I said to Jenny Baker, who was one of the other members of the Aboriginal Women's Health and Healing Project, 'Jenny, wouldn't this be fantastic to use with diabetes?' And she said, 'Yeah Barb, we should do it together'. We went away from that day with a sense of excitement, with a feeling of, 'Wow, we've got to use this'.

I couldn't wait to get to Murray Bridge, where I work, to try it. I developed an exercise which I first of all showed to the other members of the Aboriginal Women's Health and Healing Project. It worked very well and I couldn't wait to give it to the people. That was going to be the big test.

Setting the scene

In the exercise I played the role of diabetes or 'Sugar'. I carefully set the scene in ways that I felt were culturally appropriate. As an Aboriginal person I knew that it would be wrong to put other Aboriginal people on the spot, or single people out. To avoid this I came up with a number of questions that I gave to the participants which they could ask me and I would respond. The participants were very happy to start by asking these simple little questions I had already come up with. If I had expected them to come up with their own questions straight away it might have been difficult to get people to participate. Giving them questions took away the uncomfortableness. I had hoped that after they had asked me these set questions that a general conversation would begin, and this is what happened. At the end people came up with their own questions that they would have been afraid to ask at the beginning.

I had been impressed at the way the CARE counsellors of Malawi had invited communities into conversations with one character representing AIDS: Mr/Mrs AIDS, and one character representing community care: Mr/Mrs CARE. As I was doing this work on my own I only developed the one character: 'Sugar'. I thought it would be too complicated for me to play two characters, although I had seen how well this had worked in the video from Malawi. Just having the one character, 'Sugar', meant that she had to be very versatile. She spoke of the ways she was affecting people, but also at times played the role of an educator.

Perhaps we will explore using two characters later on - who knows what future directions will hold. This is just a starting point. It's not perfect. I wouldn't want to put it across as perfect. It is just to give people ideas. I want people to go off and develop their own ways of working. If it came across as perfect it could scare people - expectations might get too high. Every situation is different and every community is different. I'd like everyone to have the freedom to develop things in their own way.

Talking to 'sugar'

The group: *Who are you?*

Sugar: *My name is diabetes but a lot of people call me Sugar. You can call me I can be anybody's disease but I do my best work with Nungas[3] because they can't quite control me yet.*

There was a man in the group and when I said they could all call me Sugar it created a lot of laughter!

The group: *How do you work?*

Sugar: *It's my job to make sure you don't get enough insulin or none at all. Most people know about my condition. I'm very popular and I'm all over the world - I'm pretty sure of having a job until I retire. Years ago it was hard for me to get a job with you people because there were great hunters who lived off the land, good tucka [food] and plenty of exercise. You people were healthy. Now though, thanks to this thing called urban living, you have heaps of shops to go to and are tempted by the smell of food, by television books that always show cakes, chocolates and fatty foods. You have very little exercise. All this just makes me so happy.*

The group: *How different are you from a healthy body?*

Sugar: *To explain that I need to introduce you to my family. I come from very strong kin relationships as I know you do. Aboriginal people have strong family relationships and I totally rely on my blood relatives.*

There's my Mother Heart - without her I'm a goner, and three sets of twins - Cousin Kidneys, Cousin Pili's [eyes] and Cousin Feet except they're not here today - gone walkabout. My main man is a gland called Pancreas. This is where I do my best work. I affect all these parts of the body - all my relatives. This is what makes me different from a healthy body.

The group: *What don't you like about your job?*

Sugar: *Well I come in two types of diabetes and I don't like this part of my job.*
              I have to remember the families that have my history.

              First of all there is Type 1, or Juvenile Onset Diabetes. My work
              here is usually with young people below the age of thirty, but it can
              happen at any age. With Type 1, the pancreas produces no insulin
              because the cells that make it have been destroyed by the white cells
              of the body. People therefore require insulin injections to control
              their blood glucose levels.

              Then there is Type 2, or Mature Onset Diabetes. This usually
              happens in people who are over 40 years old and especially if they
              are overweight. Type 2 often responds to diet, appropriate exercise
              and weight reduction, but sometimes tablets and then later, insulin,
              may be required.

I would give out a handout at this point.

The group: *What makes you powerful?*

Sugar: *I become powerful when people are shamed, divided, and isolated.*
              I become powerful when people are overweight, including pregnant
              women with big babies; when Nungas over 40 never get their eyes
              tested, neglect sores, don't eat properly, don't use medication and
              injections, don't visit diabetic clinics or programs, don't have
              blood pressures taken, never have urine tests; when they do no
              exercise; and when they stay home and away from people who
              know about me.

The group: *What weakens you?*

Sugar: *It weakens me when Aboriginal people have a chance to ask questions,*
              to talk together in their own ways. It weakens me when people are no
              longer alone, when they stand together. Other things also weaken me-
              people taking responsibility for their own health, weight loss, diets,
              blood pressure checks, foot care, trachoma clinics, people controlling
              their blood sugar glucose levels. All these things weaken me.

As Sugar answers what weakens her she becomes weaker and weaker until she is almost under the table!

Different conversations

What we got out of it was quite magical. The most important thing was that, after we had been through these questions and answers, the participants started asking their own questions of Sugar. The conversations afterwards went on for an hour and a half, just discussing the issues that came up. The exercise seemed to lead to the possibility of people asking their own questions, questions that they had never felt free to ask before, and this led to new sorts of conversations.

It was obvious by the end that some people had never understood diabetes before. Maybe professional people had tried to explain and they'd been too ashamed to say 'I don't know' or, 'I don't understand'. I think we learned that we need to break diabetes down so that the people can understand.

When I asked one woman who is normally very quiet what she thought of the poster she said, 'I'd never understood what Sugar was about. That's given me a real vision.' She wasn't responding to me, she wasn't responding to the diabetic sister or the dietitian, she was responding to Sugar. It was just so different. It wasn't about me, Barb, it was because she could have a direct conversation with Sugar. Another woman was giving herself injections and she was wondering why it was so difficult. She wasn't moving the needles from place to place. We talked and talked. At the end of it I just went 'like wow!' (thumbs up)

Humour

It was really good to play Sugar. I am naturally a bit of a clown, and for a lot of Aboriginal people that is our survival tool - our humour, our joking. To create that sort of environment with Sugar was really good. They really loved it. It was because of the humour that they were able to pick it up better. The male who was there, when he sees me walking down the street, he still says, 'Here comes Sugar!' It's really rippled.

Curiosity

The relationship of the participants to Sugar was one of curiosity. Anger didn't creep in at all even when Sugar was extremely boastful. At times Sugar said really, really awful things like: 'If you don't look after your feet you'll get sores and your limbs can drop off'. After I said it I felt quite awful for saying it, but it wasn't me, it was Sugar speaking.

I think using imagery of weakening or strengthening Sugar was better than showing aggression. The idea of asking 'what makes you strong?' 'what weakens you?' was an excellent idea from the Malawi video. When Sugar was answering the question 'what weakens you?' she actually started to go down, to wilt. It was making her weak. When I ran the program here I actually got under the table - it weakened Sugar so much.

Professional relations with 'sugar'

It was wonderful to see how the other health professionals entered into a relationship with Sugar. They started to call me Sugar, and to ask questions of Sugar. To see professional people come into it and accept this whole new process, I think that warmed me the most. The diabetic sister now uses 'Sugar' in some form with mainstream clients. They have also been using the video that we made with other health professionals. The podiatrists send me very positive feedback on coloured pieces of paper in the shape of little feet! I send my notes back in black, yellow and red - Nunga coloured feet!

Culture

I wanted to bring in some cultural aspects so that they could really relate to Sugar, so they felt they belonged to Sugar. Otherwise it would have been far too mainstream and that's often the problem with other programs. That's why our people are getting lost because often there are no attempts to talk about these things in culturally appropriate ways. By talking about our people's history, we made the link between them and Sugar.

I tried to make the exercise culturally appropriate. By giving them the questions first meant that everyone was a part of the process in a non-threatening way. By not using jargon, people felt that we were all speaking the same language.

I think that often Aboriginal people have felt shamed at asking questions, or that Sugar is just too complicated to understand. The way the questions were given reduced shame - they became a part of talking with Sugar. The fact that we were talking about Nungas and our history and our culture also reduced shame.

Togetherness

Perhaps the biggest thing that reduces shame is doing something all together - breaking down the isolation. Sugar is just one of many issues facing Aboriginal people's lives. This offered a different way of seeing Sugar. They looked at Sugar that day as something that should be taken notice of, something that is affecting the Aboriginal community. It's a community problem. If it's not affecting you it's affecting your grandmother, uncle or aunty. Every family is effected by diabetes, one way or another. By all talking with Sugar it gave the feeling that together we need to take notice, and that together we can take action.

Notes

1. This chapter was first published in the 1996 No.3 issue of the *Dulwich Centre Newsletter*. It is republished here with permission.
2. In 1994 funds were allocated from the South Australian Health Commission to the National Women's Health Program to assist in the area of health and healing. With these funds an Aboriginal Women's Health Forum was established which in turn initiated the Aboriginal Women's Health and Healing Project. This project involves ten Aboriginal women from different areas within South Australia - Maggie Charles from Berri, Leta Sullivan from Goodwood, Maureen Williams from Coober Pedy, Christine Franks from Coffin Bay, Jenny Baker from Torrensville, Rosie Howson from Greenacres, Barbara Wingard from Murray Bridge, Shirley Grocke from Blyth, Terry Stewart from Angle Park and Anna Caponi from Port Augusta. The Aboriginal Women's Health and Healing Project is currently exploring a wide range of issues including training and the development of culturally appropriate ways of working.
3. See the article, 'Pang'ono pang'ono ndi·mtolo - Little by little we make a bundle: The work of the CARE Counsellors & Yvonne Sliep', in *Dulwich Centre Newsletter* 1996 No. 3

4

Lumaratjara:
Sugar in Pitjantjantjara

By

Barbara Wingard

Since the work described here in relation to 'Sugar' was first created, it has been taken up by various groups in different ways. Recently, it has been taken up by traditional Aboriginal people within the Pitjantjatjara Lands. For me, as an urban Aboriginal person, to be welcomed by these traditional people is a considerable honour. It is also a moving experience. They, of course, have retained their own language and to hear them speak brings a sense of celebration as well as a sadness in acknowledging how much many of us have lost.

Where I come from, we believe people are either Aboriginal or not Aboriginal, but on traditional lands other distinctions are often made. In the Pitjantjatjara Lands, for example, I am seen as a 'half-caste'. Even some of their own, those that are fair-skinned, they refer to as 'half-castes'. Although this way of talking and thinking is not acceptable in an urban context, or when said by non-Aboriginal people, I appreciate where the traditional people are coming from. There are very significant differences between our experiences of life and I feel it is a great honour to be welcomed by them and to be so accepted into their lives and communities.

27

As I mentioned in an earlier chapter, when I began working in a mainstream health context there were so many things which I had to adjust to as an Aboriginal person moving into a mainstream system. Now when I go into Pitjantjatjara Lands, it is a whole different context again. This time though, I am making adjustments as an urban Aboriginal person being invited onto traditional lands. There are many cultural practices to respect and it is a process that requires care. It is also great fun! To be taken out to find honey ants to eat is, for example, a real thrill. I love the country and it feels really good to be there.

The last time I travelled to Ernabella, it was with Michael White, to work with a number of traditional health workers. When they watched the Sugar video they spoke about wanting to do something in their own language, in their own way, about Sugar. After some discussion they decided to do a short video of their own in Pitjantjatjara[1]. As they worked for many hours to translate English into Pitjantjatjara, and created the script that they wanted to use, I couldn't stop smiling. It is a complex task to translate English to Pitjantjatjara as they are very different languages. There were also changes that had to be made to the original script in relation to issues of history and the local context.

When I watch their video I feel as if I am back up there with them. I also have a real sense of shared pride in the work that was done, in the sense of connection. It'll be good to hear if it has a made a difference for them, if it manages to create conversations amongst their own people. Who knows where it will go from here?

Note:

1.   The video entitled 'Lumaratjara tjukurpa' was produced by PY Media & Nganampa Health Council July 2000.

5

Externalising conversations

By

Barbara Wingard

When people hear about 'Sugar' they are often interested in how we came to work in that way. I always acknowledge that it was based on the work of the CARE Counsellors in Malawi. They were the ones who helped to give birth to 'Sugar' as they created ways of externalising HIV/AIDS in a community program.

Ideas about externalising conversations come from what is called 'narrative therapy' and they are often used in counselling. Externalising problems is about separating people from their problems. It is about taking the shame away from the person. Whatever the problem is, we try to find ways to make it separate from the person so that they can actually talk about it and resolve their own thoughts and feelings about it.

Rather than saying, 'You have diabetes', we might say 'It seems as if Sugar is trying to influence your life!'. Rather than saying 'You seem an angry person', we might ask, 'When did Anger first come into your life?'. Rather than saying, 'You are depressed', we might say 'It seems that Depression has a hold on you. Has it always been that way?'

By helping to separate people from the problems they are facing this often makes it easier to talk about them and to come up with ideas as to how to change them. I've noticed it is often easiest to understand externalising by giving an example.

The box of hurt

Not long ago I was working with a 21 year old Aboriginal lad. His relationship with his girlfriend had just ended and as a result he was heartbroken and suicidal. His mother asked me to come and see him because she was very worried. When I went around there I spent a few hours with him on the first night. I returned on the second night and after a few hours I didn't feel I was getting anywhere. He was hitting himself in the chest very forcefully. I could hear the force of the blow. And he was talking about the pain and the hurt as if it was inside of him.

One of the main aims of externalising is to find ways in which problems stop being understood as inside people, or as a part of a person. The aim is to find a way that the problem starts being seen as a separate thing. By the second evening I had really come to the end of my tether. I had a good connection with this young man but I didn't really know what to do. So I started talking about the pain and the hurt as if it was separate from him, saying things like, 'This hurt seems so powerful, so strong. What could we do with this hurt?'. I knew I needed to interrupt what was happening. After a while I thought about what you sometimes do with things you want to keep under control – you put them in a box! Explaining this, I then put my hands up in front of him as if I grabbing hold of some of his hurt and placing it in an imaginary box. I put my hands next to him like it was a box and said look, 'This is a box of your hurt. This is a box of your pain. This is where we're going to keep it'. He looked at it as if it was there, and he stopped hitting himself. It was at that moment when he looked at the box of hurt as if it was separate from himself, that he started being able to take some control over the feelings he was experiencing.

This is a bit of an dramatic example as usually externalising can take place in the ways you are speaking with someone. But in this instance this young man was past speaking. He was in a desperate state and I felt I had to take a chance to find a way of putting his pain next to him rather than inside him. I had to find a way of externalising the hurt so that we could take the problem away from the person and then talk through ways of dealing with it.

Once the problem is separate from the person that is not the end, that is just the beginning. Then you can begin to talk about the problem differently and come up with some ways of changing your relationship with the problem. This young man was able to do this. It wasn't that he no longer felt any pain or hurt, but he could control it better now. He knew there were times that he could place it in the box and get on with other aspects of his life. He got better quite quickly after that evening, and when he was feeling much happier he came up to me and said, 'I will never forget the box of pain.' He had thought the pain was inside of him, inside his chest, where he kept hitting himself. He thought the pain and the hurt was a part of him, that this was all he was. Moving the pain and the hurt to somewhere else made other things possible.

In the previous chapter, 'Sugar' was an example of an externalising conversation. 'The box of hurt' is a different sort of example. There are many others[1].

Note:
1. If you want to read more about externalising conversations or narrative therapy please see 'What is narrative therapy? An easy-to-read introduction' by Alice Morgan (Dulwich Centre Publications 2000).

6

Rekindling family – responding to violence in Aboriginal families

By

Jane Lester

Many years ago, in the late 1980s, I was doing child care work at the Rape Crisis Centre here in Adelaide when I attended a three day conference on domestic violence. During those three days I was shocked as each presenter painted different pictures of what had gone on in my family while I was growing up. I found myself thinking that if this had gone on in our family, and I knew it also had gone on in many other Aboriginal families, then something had to be done about it.

The early days

I thought that the first step would be to create some avenues of support for children who were moving through the child protection system because of some violation in their family context, and I began talking about this with those around me. In response, someone suggested that I should write a submission and send it off to the government departments in order to establish a counsellor position for kids in relation to their experiences of violence in the home. I'd never written a submission before in my life, and I hadn't worked a great deal outside of the home either. I was doing child care work at Rape Crisis Centre, and had just started a traineeship. One day, as I was walking out the front door, I sang out to the administrator, 'how do you write a submission?'. She replied 'Oh, you need an introduction, you need to justify what you're asking for, you need to offer some background to the issue, you throw in some statistics, write a conclusion and include a budget.' I thought 'oh, all right', and so I went home and started piecing all this together. It seemed relatively straight forward so I got the submission written and sent it off to all government departments. Years later I discovered that this submission had created a bit of a stir because it didn't come on letterhead! It was just from this woman called Jane Lester! I imagine a lot of the people who read it thought 'who the hell is she?!'. Anyway, it must have gone around the traps because I received a phone call saying that I needed to go and find an organisation to auspice the money. Having found an organisation, and re-submitted the submission, we received the funding!

Because I had been working in the Rape Crisis Centre, I knew that Aboriginal women were not accessing that service, or other mainstream services, and that there were a number of reasons why. My initial job was to try to make these services more accessible to the Aboriginal community. And so I began to speak publicly about issues of domestic violence, rape and child sexual abuse in Aboriginal families. These were still very taboo subjects at the time. I remember the first time I spoke on these issues at the Aboriginal Women's National Conference here in South Australia. It was the first time that these issues had been discussed in such a forum and I had a lot of people come up to me beforehand and say 'Geez you've got guts going up there talking about that. I reckon there'll be some rotten tomatoes and rotten eggs coming your way". Before too long I was feeling petrified! But I calmed down when I realised that my Aunty was going to be the chair of the session. What really astonished me was that when I looked down into the crowd before I began to speak I saw six Aunties all sitting in a row waiting to catch my eye – they were all waving. I thought to myself, 'I hope they're not doing that when I get up there to talk, or I'll lose the plot!' It was so beautiful. I'd practised so many times that I managed to get it all out. There were no rotten tomatoes and no rotten eggs, just a helluva lot of clapping. Everyone seemed so relieved that we were finally talking about these issues. Hearing my Aunties say, 'You did a good job' and 'You're on the right track, go for it' meant a lot to me. Especially as many of them at that stage didn't have any idea what my childhood had been like.

That was the beginning. So many different projects began after that. An Aboriginal film crew was funded to go around Australia and look at what's actually happening in the community with regard to domestic violence. They made a video and through this process I met the woman who was to become my mentor around these issues. It was she who introduced me to the term 'family violence' and encouraged me to look at the issues in a broad context instead of breaking them up into domestic violence, into rape, into child sexual abuse. The phrase 'family violence' acknowledges that violence can happen to anyone within the family unit, and that if violence is occurring it affects everybody in the family. Then in 1990 the National Report on violence in Australia found that Aboriginal women are ten times more likely to die through homicide than non-Aboriginal women. As an Aboriginal woman I found this quite horrifying. From discussions since, I've learnt that this statistic is simply an average which means that in some places the figures are much worse, and in others much better. In the Kimberley region at one stage I believe that Aboriginal women were over thirty times more likely to be victims of homicide than any other member of the Australian community. These are quite shocking statistics.

With the new found awareness of the issue, funding was made available and we began the process of setting up a three-year pilot program. But I didn't want this job. I wanted to have more babies! When I spoke with my family however they all said, 'No, you're not having a baby, you're gonna do this job. That's your next step. Take the opportunity while it's there'. And so I did, although there were all sorts of dilemmas, primarily practical ones. The funding body wanted the program to be held in Pt Augusta, but I didn't want to take my eight year old to live there as it is very racist town. She'd been raised with a very positive perspective of culture, her Aboriginality, and I didn't want this crushed. We worked out that she would stay in Adelaide while I worked in Port Augusta. I would commute home on weekends.

It's a reality that it's very hard to run intense programs like those addressing issues of family violence and run a family at the same time. One always loses out, and generally it's your own family. It is a difficult issue to resolve as an Aboriginal woman - how to work on the broader issues and try to address the difficulties that all Aboriginal families are having, and, at the same time, how to work to ensure your own family is in good shape and that your children's spirits are protected from the harshness of mainstream culture. This has been a significant struggle for me.

And yet, we set up the program in Port Augusta and later we established the Family Training, Education, Awareness and Resource Centre in Adelaide. This was the South Australian branch of the National Family Violence Intervention Program and I was the State Coordinator. We were involved in developing training for Aboriginal staff, community education with a focus on marriage counseling, workshops in schools, and reaching out to prisoners who had been convicted of acts of violence. We established support systems for children experiencing domestic violence, and support groups for women, men and children as well as counselling for young victims. We also provided Aboriginal cultural support groups and programs. We were determined to create these services with integrity to Aboriginal cultural ways and so established an Aboriginal Advisory Group to assist in this process.

A community issue

In addressing violence within the Aboriginal community we use the term 'family violence' as we acknowledge that Aboriginal men, woman and children are all affected in some form or another. In addressing this issue I believe that it important to acknowledge that violence is not just a women's issue but a community issue. That's not to say that sometimes women won't need to meet separately over these issues, or men won't need to meet separately, but everything has to happen from a community awareness perspective. We have to join together to address this issue. Perhaps the clearest way of conveying this is that it is no longer just 'them killing us' but we are also killing ourselves. There have been more family violence deaths in one Aboriginal community alone than there were Aboriginal deaths in custody cases presented to the Royal Commission. Finding ways of addressing this violence is a community issue of the highest importance.

Connecting with history

In order to address this violence we are going to need to understand its historical context. I think it's important to connect people with how the history of this country has impacted on Aboriginal communities and how family violence fits in relation to this history. Any community that has experienced dispossession, injustice, hardshipand division is likely to react with a sense of outrage and anger. When communities are relatively powerless, the easiest people to take this anger and rage out on are those closest to you.

This acknowledgement of history is important because it means that we are all in it together. But this history is not an excuse. It is the opposite. This history can act as an invitation to be a part in creating a future of our people free from violence rather than a part of further perpetuating the violence that we have been subjected to for so long. Talking about history gives people a chance to understand what is happening all around them. It offers people a chance to separate who they are, and who they want to be, from violence and to clarify what they want to offer in terms of the future of Aboriginal communities.

It is relevant that many of those who perpetrate violence in our communities were the victims of violence in their own childhoods. The learning of violence is in some ways generational. Ways of being violent are being handed down from generation to generation. But this violence is not an Aboriginal tradition. It is a legacy of what has been done to Aboriginal people. Making this distinction is important. Acknowledging the history of this country and how it contributes to violence in Aboriginal families, and recognising the difference between legacies of violence and Aboriginal traditions can show us ways forward.

This has been very significant for me personally. In order to understand what happened in our family I have had to understand my father's life, and I can only do that through understanding the history of this country and policies of assimilation. He lived a life constrained by the effects of government policy and this affected all of our family life. By understanding his life in context I can see that the violence in our home came from my father being disconnected from his family, from his community and from ways of living that would have fitted with Aboriginal traditions of respect.

Once we begin to see that family violence is not something that we can keep quiet and secret, once we see that it occurs in a historical context, then we can begin the task of reconnecting with Aboriginal traditions of respect. This is a different sort of reconnecting with history.

Reclaiming culture and respectful traditions

In pre-colonial times Aboriginal cultures had developed intricate practices of respect and ways of living in harmony with the land and with each other. Our work to address family violence involves reclaiming this harmony. It is about reclaiming self and for Aboriginal people this means reclaiming family, reclaiming culture, reclaiming community, and reclaiming connection to land.

Family violence is a sickness of the lost. Alcoholism is a sickness of the lost. Substance abuse is a sickness of the lost. Due to the process of colonisation there are many Aboriginal people who don't even know where their country is, where they come from, who their mob is. For Aboriginal people that is a violation to self, it's a form of family violence in itself. In all of our programs, groups and counselling we are interested in finding ways for Aboriginal people to come home to culture and community, and to come home to traditions and practices of respect that offer other ways of living in families.

As I have written in other chapters, I myself have had to go through the long process of reconnecting with my people, culture and land. It is process that will never end. But there are significant markers along the way. When I introduce myself now and say 'My name is Jane Lester, and I'm a *Yangkuntjatjara / Antakarinya* woman', there is a hum of connectedness with others in the room. It's like putting your snow skis on, you click your feet in, and you're ready to go! When my youngest child was born we placed her feet straight into red dirt from our traditional lands. These are all steps to redress the violence done to our families, and they are steps to prevent further violence.

Through the eyes of children

These days I am working from home so that I can care for my youngest daughter. I see this as ongoing work in reclaiming and prioritising family life and our future generations. Caring for our children was the primary theme that informed our conversations with the community in relation to family violence. It is children who carry the memory of violence the longest, and it is our children who will be creating our future families. In our workshops we would always invite adults to consider the perspectives of children, to think about what our children are seeing, what they are learning. Talking from the perspectives of children would generally get everybody listening, including the men. Often it would invite people to remember their own childhoods.

Within our group programs we would invite people to consider the historical perspective of family violence, and then the future perspective through the eyes of our children. This way it would become clear that it's our responsibility as individuals and as families to create changes so that violence is not handed on from one generation to the next. I would often share my own story. I would talk about my childhood and my young adult life. I would explain that the whole reason I became involved in this area is that after attending that first domestic violence conference all those years ago, I could see that in some ways I was duplicating to my first child what had been done to me. I didn't want to go down that road. Getting involved in trying to address family violence was like saying 'Stop. Let's do a re-check'. I think talking about my own struggles and experiences encouraged a lot of other people to start talking about their lives. It helps people to realise that they are not alone. And we aren't alone on this issue! Family violence is affecting so many of our families.

The future

Just this week I was invited to join a reference group that's putting together a national family violence conference next year here in Adelaide. The title of the conference is 'Rekindling Family'. It's a three-day event and the first day is all about acknowledging country and our connections to land. This is the direction in which we are now moving. We are realising that addressing violence is going to involve rekindling family relations, rekindling Aboriginal traditions and relationships of respect, and reconnecting with country.

We have to come up with solutions, with ways to guide our people away from violence and back to respectful ways. The violence that is happening in Aboriginal families is so serious that we are all going to have to play a part in addressing it. One thing that I think I have inherited from being a second generation mission child, is faith. I have faith that things can change, that little miracles breeze in the door when you most need them. I have faith that we can turn things around. Then again, another legacy of the mission days is a belief in hard work. I have faith that through hard work we can turn things around.

7

Finding our own
ways to grieve,
to remember and to heal

by

Barbara Wingard

Grief's presence has been with us for a very long time. As Aboriginal people we have had too many losses. Sometimes it seems as if we are moving from one death to another. Our people just get so weary that at times it's too much to go to one more funeral. We simply have to find ways of grieving together because it's far too hard to do it on our own.

We are seeking ways of speaking about Grief that are consistent with our cultural ways of doing things. We are remembering those who have died, we are honouring Indigenous spiritual ways, and we are finding ways of grieving that bring us together.

Dealing with our grief, with all of the losses we have experienced, is not about moving on and forgetting. It's about remembering our people and bringing them with us wherever we go. I've lost a brother, my father, my grandmother and many others, but I believe that they're still with me. I carry a lot of their ways. I acknowledge them.

These days, if you talk too much about the past, people look at you as a radical - they think you're trying to stir up trouble There are those who say, 'We've got to forget about the past and move on'. That's fine to a point, but I think we have to acknowledge the events that happened in the past that had an impact on our grandparents, our parents, and, whether we acknowledge it or not, on ourselves. When people say, 'Forget the past', they're asking us to leave a lot behind. They're asking us to desert our old folks. We cannot move on and leave them behind - we must bring them with us wherever we go. Our old people are who we belong to.

When a people has had as many losses as we have had, it is not time to forget and move on. It is time to remember, to stay connected to our people, past and present. We will not forget our people and we will not forget the past. We have to acknowledge and keep on acknowledging all that has happened in this country.

Reconnecting with our own healing ways

We are trying to listen to people's stories to put them more in touch with their own healing ways.

My father died when I was 14, and I remember seeing him in the coffin. I wanted to cry out loud and yet the environment that we were in didn't allow for me to grieve in my way. I think European society has encouraged particular ways of grieving and they don't necessarily fit for Aboriginal people. If you go to a funeral service in an Aboriginal community you can wail and cry and grieve the way you want to grieve. But in mainstream funeral services there seems to be a lot of silent grieving.

I don't believe that this silence fits with Aboriginal culture. I don't believe that this silence is a good thing. I especially don't think it's good for our young men. Some of the women perhaps have a better mechanism because they have a network in which they're not afraid to shed tears. But silent cries can go on for years and be heard by no-one. They can eat away at a person's spirit.

If only all those people who are silently crying could find ways to come together. I think they'd be quite amazed how much they have in common and how much they'd want to share somebody else's story.

We are trying to find ways to bring together our people who are grieving. At Camp Coorong, in 1994, all Aboriginal families in South Australia who had experienced a death in custody gathered together to talk about the links between grief, loss and injustice and to try to find culturally appropriate ways forward. The document that came from this gathering was called 'Reclaiming Our Stories, Reclaiming Our Lives' (1995).

Here is an extract from it:

> *Aboriginal people have always had their own special ways of healing. This includes ways of healing the pain from loss and injustice.*
>
> *These healing ways have been disrespected by non-Aboriginal people, and Aboriginal people have been discouraged from using them. But the healing ways have survived and are playing an important part in Aboriginal life today.*
>
> *Talking together more about the healing ways is one path to taking them back, to making them stronger.* (p.15)

More recently we have held a further gathering in an Aboriginal community in northern NSW to try to create a context in which family members who had tragically lost children could come together and find ways of healing. Some of the healing ways that this community spoke about included 'Aboriginal spirituality', 'Connection to the land', 'Relationships with elders', 'Keeping memories alive' and 'Sharing stories that unite'.

These gatherings are one way in which we are trying to address grief in Aboriginal communities We are also exploring special ways of remembering that make it possible for people to see themselves through the eyes of their lost loved ones.

Special ways of remembering

Finding ways to bring people with us, those who are no longer living can make a big difference to people's lives. When we reconnect with those we have lost, and the memories we have forgotten, then we become stronger. When we see ourselves through the loving eyes of those who have cared for us our lives are easier to live.

When people are going through hard times often the conversations that are important involve reconnecting with earlier loving moments and bringing back people's fathers, mothers, grandparents into their lives. Sometimes just remembering one special moment can be really significant, especially if the memory can be described in detail.

Recently, I remember speaking to a man who was very angry with his Dad who had died years ago. Gradually we brought his father to our conversations, let him join us, and as we did he recalled a specific event. He remembered a day in the lands when it was raining. His father had found shelter for them both and had placed his arms around him for comfort and warmth. Somehow, remembering this single scene changed everything, for as the son saw himself through the eyes of his father, he reconnected with his father's love. He reconnected with the knowledge that his father must have loved him. So many stories of this love had been forgotten, and as he sat there retelling them I watched a weight lift from him. It was almost like Mr Anger just jumped out of his body and I was looking at a different person. His expression was so soft as he spoke of wanting to share these stories of his father with his brothers and his sisters. I don't know where Mr Anger went, but it was beautiful to watch him go. It was beautiful to witness a reconciliation between father and son.

Whether we are meeting with individuals or with communities, finding ways to assist people get in touch with their own ways of grieving, their own ways of remembering and their own ways of healing seems so important. Finding ways of assisting people to maintain connection with their lost loved ones will hopefully mean that they have a little more company as they walk into the future.

Reference

Aboriginal Health Council of South Australia, 1995:

　'Reclaiming Our Stories, Reclaiming Our Lives.' *Dulwich Centre Newsletter*, 1.

8

Grief:
Remember, reflect, reveal[1]

by

Barbara Wingard

Grief is an area that we have so much work to do on in Aboriginal communities. It's hard for us to develop programs in a lot of areas, including talking about diabetes or heart disease, if there is so much grief in our communities. So many of our losses have been unjust and unacknowledged, and because of this they can be difficult to deal with, difficult to grieve. For a long time I have been interested in trying to find ways of talking with Aboriginal people about these issues. This year, issues of grief once again touched my own life when I heard about the West Terrace Project.

West Terrace Project

In our day if you had a stillborn baby, or a baby that died soon after birth, the health professionals would remove the baby and take care of all the arrangements. The mother often wouldn't even see the baby's body and they wouldn't know where the body was taken. The West Terrace Project has involved trying to find the location of the graves of these children. There had been many, many enquiries over the years about where the babies had been buried. Apparently there were so many enquiries that they found there were 30,000 babies supposed to be buried at West Terrace Cemetery. People wanted to know where. I was one of these mothers. I lost my son Michael shortly after his birth. I didn't know where he was buried and so I got involved in the West Terrace Project. I attended the ceremony of the unveiling of the Baby Memorial that is dedicated to all the lost children.

West Terrace Cemetery, Adelaide
Baby Memorial

Under a Bay tree, a small sitting space formed by a curved wall of quarried stone which directs attention to a symbolic bowl of water made of granite on which floats a broken chain of white daisies in bronze. The water symbolises calm, the white daisies innocence and the broken chain - a life cut off. The plaques are in the shape of leaves set in ceramic tiles and the whole memorial is in the form of a carpet of bay leaves - bay leaves do not change when they fall.

(Extract from Dedication and Unveiling of the Baby Memorial. West Terrace Cemetery, Adelaide, South Australia. Sunday, March 10th, 1996)

When I went to the ceremony at the West Terrace Cemetery I didn't see any Aboriginal women at the unveiling, and it bothered me. I thought that out of 30,000 babies there must be Aboriginal babies out there. Where were the people? That made me think that we need to get out there and talk, spread the word, share with them about the West Terrace Project. So I began to tell my story and send information out to other Aboriginal women.

Speaking out

As I was doing this I was asked to present at the Stillbirth and Neo Natal Deaths (SANDS) Conference. I agreed. I thought it would be an opportunity for me to share my story which would be healing for me, and I also wanted to tell the stories of Aboriginal people. I knew that I'd be the only Aboriginal person at the conference.

I wished that there would be more of us but I also knew how daunting these conferences can be for me.

I decided to try to use my own grief as a way of joining. We all had that in common. I thought I could tell my own story of grief and then make the links to the broader stories of grief that we as Aboriginal people have experienced. I thought it might be healing for all of us. I began by telling my own story.

My story as an Aboriginal woman: The loss of a twin in the 1960s

Today I am going to share a part of my life with you and reflect on what it was like for me as a sixteen year old in the 1960s. In those days we had an Aborigines Act where some Aboriginal people were given an Exemption which allowed us to mix with the wider community, but it also indicated that we ceased to be Aboriginal.

This act prevented many of my people from returning to their birth places on the missions. Also there was a loitering act which prevented people of many different races congregating together. This included mixing with our own people as well as our white friends.

In those days, we were not even citizens of this country. This didn't happen until 1967 when we could vote. As a young girl growing up in these times I had a sense of not belonging and trying to hang on to my identity. During my school days I failed to fit in to the school system and spent my time in a special class till I was thirteen, and was able to get myself a job in a factory. It was good to get away from being called 'blacky' and 'dummy'. By this time I figured out that I didn't have anything in that head of mine but there wasn't anything wrong with my hands. By the time I was sixteen I felt like an old woman and fell in love and became pregnant ... even got married. But, like many Aboriginal women, I didn't like Doctors and Hospitals. After all, I wasn't sick. Pregnancy to me wasn't a sickness, it was a natural condition.

After getting a bit of pressure from my mother to book into the hospital, I decided to go there seven months into my pregnancy. During the birth it was noticed that I was delivering twins, both boys. The first twin was 7lbs, the second was only 3lbs 14oz and he was breech, plus he had chest complications. I remember the joy of having two sons.

Two days later my son, Michael, passed away. I was young and death scared me and I wasn't encouraged to talk about it. The hospital took care of the burial which was to be at West Terrace Cemetery. There were no funeral services in those days. I had a baby to take home. My other son, Shawn, has been a constant reminder all these years and always will be, but that was the practice then - how times have changed!

Then early this year, I found out through the media about the project known as the Baby Memorial at West Terrace Cemetery which had been prompted by the requests of grieving mothers.

It was then that I was able to cry again. I couldn't believe that after all this time that I had unresolved grief. I felt disbelief - I am a Health Worker and know all about grief and the process... I couldn't help thinking about the mass graves. Going to the Baby Memorial Service was a great relief to me and my children.

After the service I needed to know where Michael's resting place was, but, following many enquiries, I found that he wasn't even at the West Terrace Cemetery!!!! At this stage I decided to write my story for other Aboriginal women and give them information and details of the West Terrace project.

A very special thankyou to the researchers at the West Terrace Cemetery, for their dedication and compassion for this project.

A happy ending for my story is that I have found out, finally, almost 32 years to the day, where my son is buried: the Cheltenham Cemetery was my son's last journey, his resting place.

Telling my story

Talking about my own story first was a bit emotional for me. I'd only just found out where Michael was buried. It was a bit emotional and that was clear in my voice. The Stillbirth and Neo Natal Death Support conference was a very moving time for a lot of women who had lost their babies. Women were finally talking. So many of us had been told not to, that it might upset us. A lot of the mothers who had lost their babies had been told: 'You've got to let go and move on now'. And that's the worst thing you can say. There is a lot of pressure to grieve in particular ways. We are trying to challenge this. We are trying to allow people to grieve in their own ways. Now we are talking, following it through.

My story was an old story, my loss. I used it as an indicator of how long grief can be with us. I also used that story to show that it wasn't just about my grief, that it's also about Aboriginal people and our 'griefs', all the different sorts of losses and injustices that we are trying to find our ways through.

At the SANDS conference there were no Aboriginal people except myself. I told my story in a way to let them know what it was like in the days when we weren't citizens of this country, when we couldn't vote. I told my story in these ways because we're always trying, us guys, always trying to get them to understand!

Telling my own story of grief was a way of joining with the non-Aboriginal people there. In some way I saw that grief could help us join - to create the context for us to talk through the broader losses. I wanted to talk about injustice in a healing way because, for us as Aboriginal people, telling the stories of injustice is a part of our grieving, a part of honouring our histories. Once I had told my story I thought, 'Okay that's my story. I've made the connection with the audience, now to move on, to let people know what it's like for us as Aboriginal people.'

Externalizing 'grief'

I had decided that I would try to play the character of 'Grief' and to invite the audience to ask me particular questions. I knew this would be very different to externalizing AIDS or Sugar, but I thought that it might help us to find common ground from where I could share the experiences of Aboriginal people. I wanted to make sure we could talk about our losses and injustices as Aboriginal people in a healing way. Playing the character of Grief and giving the participants questions to ask me was just a starting point. I'm telling this story in the hope that it will give people ideas that they could work on, so that they can come up with their own ways of working.

Talking with 'grief'

The group: *Have we met you before? What is your name?*

Grief: *Yes, you could have come across me sometime in your lives, in one way or another. My name is Grief and I'm the response to loss. I'm a process or a way of doing things.*

The group: *Has your presence been with Aboriginal People?*

Grief: *Yes and for a long time. To give you a good picture, allow me to take you on a Journey of Aboriginal History through some of the events in this country's past (loss of land, sickness, deaths, health, loss of language). You need to read in-between the lines for many happenings: removal of children, deaths in custody, rights and culture.*

At this point I put up a poster of the 'Journey of Aboriginal History' (see page 51) and encouraged people to fill in the gaps on the poster which I had left blank.

The group: *What's your way of doing things?*

Grief: *Let me talk about the different ways that people relate to me. I'm like stepping stones, and people step differently.*

When I spoke about stepping stones I talked in my own language and had a dialogue with the audience. I tried to talk about stepping stones from an Aboriginal perspective. One of the ways I did this was to focus on little griefs as with death all around us sometimes it is too overwhelming to talk about at first.

Aboriginal ways of grieving

Aboriginal people have their own ways of grieving. A part of Aboriginal people's story telling is that we hold onto our loved ones that aren't here any longer. It is a part of our history, who we belong to, who we are related to - our ancestors.

When an Aboriginal person meets another Aboriginal person we work out how we know each other through our relatives. We often refer to people who are no longer alive. Our old people are still very much with us. Through them we identify each other. I might not know your parents, but who were their parents? We constantly reflect and remember these people.

All my histories are through my grandmother. Everybody knows of her and her children. Hanging on to those old people is very much part of our strength. It is a part of our story-telling. They are talked about and so they are still with us.

When I talked about stepping stones it was with the hope that this metaphor would give a sense of movement, a sense of where people have been at and where

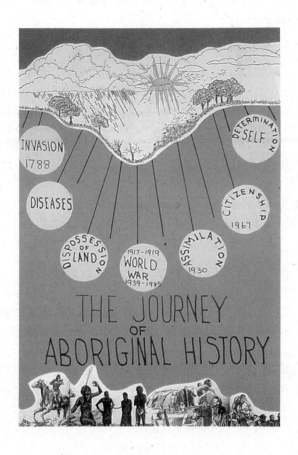

Aboriginal History

'Let me take you on a journey

of Aboriginal history'

they might move. We discussed the many different reactions people can have to loss. We talked about finding our own ways, our own individual ways, and our own cultural ways of grieving.

The group: *How close is loss to you?*

Grief: *Very close - we are partners. As I said before, Grief is the response to loss. Let me give you a definition of loss: 'It's something or someone you had or loved that has gone out of your lives'. People don't fully understand how broad loss is. Let me share with   you the many different losses and you may be able to reflect on the Journey of Aboriginal History and the Journey of Grief.*

At this point I tried to invite people to consider the losses and injustices that we as Aboriginal people have experienced and how we are trying to come to terms with these.

The group: *How can we deal with you?*

Grief: *There are many ways, people do it differently. Some people do it through having support available, talking about their grief, through maintaining spiritual and religious beliefs, through expressing feelings and stories - Men it's okay to cry. Some people help by gently encouraging the person to tell his/her own story, through listening far more than they talk. Never try to measure another person's grief. Their grief is what they say it is. Treat with love and respect any person who is grieving. Remember that every individual will grieve in their own way.*

The beginnings of a conversation

It was a very moving experience. By starting on what we had in common it allowed me to share broader stories in a powerful way, a joined way. People were very open. It was wonderful to talk with the non-Aboriginal people afterwards. They were coming up to talk and hear more. I think it is good for non-Aboriginal people to hear these stories from Aboriginal people in the ways that we choose to tell them. It invites them to understand what has happened to Aboriginal people. It seemed as if a conversation had begun, a conversation that could be healing for all of us.

A different feeling

The session had a whole different feeling to Sugar (see chapter 3). Grief is such a sensitive issue so I did it in very different ways. I couldn't use humour. I couldn't be boastful. It was difficult as I had to shift from being silly and yet still get the message across. I love being boastful and silly and making people laugh. The humour was the one thing I did miss. Grief isn't a funny thing. It is a sad and delicate thing. We can't be laughing about it.

Honouring grief, talking together

I feel very close to Grief for lots and lots of reasons. I think the young children that we have now, the youth, really need to be in touch with our histories, including our histories of loss and how we have dealt with them. In some ways it is honouring of our grief. I wanted to get over to the people that grief is natural, normal, a thing that we have to go through. A lot of our people don't want to talk about Grief as we've had a lot of losses. Often it seems as if we are just moving from one death to another. Sometimes our people just get so weary. Sometimes it's just too much to go to one more funeral.

We have to find ways of grieving together. It's far too hard to do on our own. I wanted us to look at Grief together, in a positive way, not a negative way but in a way that names the injustices, acknowledges our dead, and honours Aboriginal ways. I wanted to acknowledge that people grieve in different ways, and also to acknowledge the light at the end of the tunnel. I think the externalizing gave a little bit of a vision - that there's room to move on. That there are ways to deal with Grief together.

Grieving in our own ways

Aboriginal people have many different ways of dealing with grief. Often when people die there can be a good feeling that their spirit will be going with all the other spirits, other lost loved ones. A lot of Aboriginal people experience signs from loved ones who have died. Seeing particular birds, for instance, is often experienced as having ongoing contact with people who have died, ongoing contact with their spirits.

Some people feel that they have to move house after a person has died because their loved one's spirit still lives in the building. When I lost a loved one I needed to get the room in which he died blessed before I could re-enter it. There are a lot of different ways that Aboriginal people grieve. They can be quite complex.

I hope that the exercise and these ways of talking about grief puts people more in touch with their own ways of relating to death, to grief, to loss. I hope that it puts people more in touch with their own healing ways. I think telling the story of my own grief gives people a chance to relate to stories of loss and how differently they can be dealt with over time.

Reflecting on cultural histories

I am interested in using these ways of working with Aboriginal people. I think externalizing grief could invite people to reflect on their culture. A lot of programs don't reflect on Aboriginal culture and don't include our history. Many people are starting to forget about the invasion and the losses we have had: the land, the language, the culture. I want to talk about grief in ways that invite our people to reflect on our histories. Not to dwell on the past but to remember it, to look at some of the issues, some of the events in their lives, and see them as stepping stones. We need to talk about our history with our own people otherwise we are going to lose our young ones. They're going to have a lot of identity problems about where they belong and where they fit, and we have to help them. I think we do.

For Aboriginal people in some ways inviting people into conversations with Grief is inviting people to hold on. Grief invites us to cherish our people and histories. We need situations that invite us to be in touch with our histories to keep them alive. Talking about losses in these ways is one way of keeping our stories alive.

I'm trying to find ways for my people not to be angry, but, at the same time, I want us to understand our anger - deaths in custody, babies taken from families - there are many reasons. I want us to reflect on those histories - look at them as losses in our lives, and remember. Because we've started forgetting. Our culture is constantly being challenged, and this way our people can remember and reflect.

Grief and justice

It is important for us as Aboriginal people to make the links between justice and grief. So many of our losses have been unjust, and this is what is so hard to deal with. So many of our deaths are due to injustice. We are losing a lot of our people well before their time. A lot of our deaths are not natural deaths - for example, deaths in custody. It is tragic that we are losing our people so young. When my father died he was thirty-nine, a week off his fortieth birthday. To us that is a tragic event, but it is a common one. People like me, who are nearly fifty, we count our blessings that we are here each day. We say to each other how lucky we are to still be alive. We don't take life for granted. We need the injustices addressed so that we can grieve our losses. We need stories told and acknowledged. Working on our grief in these ways is working towards justice.

Futures

I've been Sugar, I've been Grief. I can't wait for another one now - to see what it might be. There is so much work to be done at a grassroots level, and there are lots of other workers who are interested in building on this sort of work. It all blended in beautifully. And my own story of grief had a happy ending. I found my baby just before I went to the SANDS conference. A week before the conference they rang me up to tell me they had found him at Cheltenham Cemetery. So we're going to get a little plaque now. That's our next step - to have a family gathering to say goodbye to him, to honour him.

It was moving for me to find a way to be joined on issues of grief across cultures that got us talking together. It was also powerful to realise the links in my own life. There were many links for me between finding my way through my own losses and injustices, such as where my baby had been buried, and getting in touch with ways of working with Aboriginal communities on the injustices and losses we have all experienced. They were linked in some way. The link is there. I had to tell my story - to share it. We have to share our stories - to grieve and honour. We have to tell our stories in ways that make us stronger.

Note
1. This chapter was first published in the 1996 No.3 issue of the *Dulwich Centre Newsletter*. It is republished here with permission.

9

Family equals people, land and language

By

Jane Lester

I'd like to dedicate this chapter to my grandmother who had all seven of her children taken away. She lost each of her children, including my father, in four different batches of abduction - each by the Protector of Aborigines, each sanctioned by the Australian Government of the day. According to the people of the central deserts, from where my grandmother came, our grandmothers and the crow are one. And so to begin this paper, I would like to invite you on a journey on the wings of a crow. I'd like you to imagine that you are high above this country, so high that you can look down and view its history. As you soar above this land taking in its vast horizons, I'd like you to imagine the different peoples who have lived with this country for thousands upon thousands of years. I'd like you to consider what it means to live on a land which holds the oldest living culture on earth. And as I take you with me through some of the histories of my own family, and tell stories of loss and stories of pride, I'd like you to view them from the perspective of our grandmothers, from the wings of the crow.

To begin though, I'd like to talk a little about history itself. Whether we are Indigenous to this land or not, I believe our culture and our histories are shaping our lives in the present in ways in which often we do not notice. The roads we are walking are not as new as we believe them to be. There is, I believe, an extraordinary richness to be found in exploring how our past and present are linked.

For me, the histories I wish to explore are those of my grandparents on my father's side - grandparents whom I never met. As I was growing up I knew my mother's parents and I would ask about my father's. He would say to me simply, 'They are finished. They are not around anymore'. When I would ask, 'when did they die?', my father would reply, 'I don't know'. As result of government policy my father did not know when his parents died, or where they lay.

My father and his seventeen cousins made up one entire mission home. They were separated from family, from language, from land and not surprisingly this profoundly effected the person he became. I last saw my father when I was thirteen and he died three years later. I grew up knowing little about dad's side of the family, the blackfella side, and yet on the non-Aboriginal side we were very strong in family connection. In the late 1950s, four generations of us were living on one site. We were raised knowing our Ewen Family history who settled at Encounter Bay in 1836.

Ironically, my non-Aboriginal family had more black faces amongst us than white, as mum's parents adopted four Aboriginal kids, and their first two biological children married Aboriginal men and they fostered many Aboriginal kids of all ages. There were always many children around and a great mixture of languages. I now know that one of the languages that was often spoken was from my country, but I didn't know this at the time as I didn't know where my father had come from.

Finding out about my father's family has required years of searching, but in the process I have come home. I now know that I am a Yankunytjatjara / Antakarinya woman, a descendent of desert peoples as well of Europe. I am now learning of my father's people, their land, and its language.

Re-making connections with my blackfella history is very different than seeking out my non-Aboriginal family tree. On my whitefella side, with a quick journey through the internet or the state library I can find dates and names travelling back generations, but it is much harder to find meaningful stories. My challenge then is to build stories around the names and dates, to try to understand the context of their lives. Only through these explorations can my European ancestors come to life in my mind. Only through this process can I have any chance to understand how their values and attitudes were passed from generation to generation. I can start with names and dates and then build the stories.

On the blackfella side we start with stories. Names and dates can't be a focus because often they can't be found. Dates or records in that sense were never a key element of our society. So then what do we look for? The fragments of stories, and the people who can tell us them. Some of the stories we listen for are about the times in which our parents and grandparents lived. We learn what their lives would have been like and how the histories of this country and government policies dictated which dreams our families could fulfil and which they could not.

Sometimes, once we start looking, our histories and our families seek us out. Twelve years ago, for instance, I was sitting with 120 others at Uluru when I was picked out by older women and men when they recognised me as family. 'That's a Lester sitting there', they said. At the time I had assumed that my Aunty had introduced me to them but when I went to thank her at the end of our journey a week later, she looked at me blankly and said, 'I never told them that you were there. They came and told me to bring you to them. They knew who you were.' An event like that heals the heart and the spirit. For many of us who have known we were Aboriginal but have not known where we came from, to be recognised by family is a validation that there is after all somewhere we belong. After years of doubt and being unable to answer questions about my Aboriginality, I cannot convey what being recognised by family meant to me.

Since then there have been many similar events, but there has also been hard work searching for connections. Over the years we have pieced together many stories, particularly about my grandfather. We have found old ten pound lease documents to stinking hot country miles out of any township, land in which if you don't know what you are doing you are finished. We have also found handwritten letters by my grandfather – just to see his handwriting brings a closer connection. Through those letters I have read of his life and delighted in the small stories – the time that he lost his camels on the way to the June mail for example. In hearing these stories and re-telling them to others, Charles Lester has become a person I feel I now know. I have also learnt that he was very protective of his seven children. He didn't want the mission to have anything to do with them and would hide the kids out bush when he knew the missionaries were coming. I have found his actions very beautiful. I have also found it amazing that these missionaries tracked throughout this country in horse and buggy. When you go out there and you are in a motor vehicle it is huge country, huge and hot. To imagine the missionaries doing all they did on horse and bloody cart, is incredible. All in the name of the Lord!

It took some looking but we also found out where my father's father is buried. Through my aunties and the Alice Springs Council I discovered that Charles Lester is buried in the Alice Springs cemetery. With this discovery, I can now answer at least half the question that I used to ask my dad. I have found my grandfather. We are still looking for my grandmother. My nieces and various older women out bush are trying to find out where she might be buried.

Tracing family histories for us as Aboriginal people involves more than finding our relatives and their stories. It also means coming home to country. Travelling the same old tracks that my grandparents used to travel on their camels, visiting the rock holes where they once would have rested, and learning the stories of their land, reconnects me to history in a physical sense. This is a reconnection that makes all the difference. I am hoping that in time we will find a particular location within the traditional lands where future generations of Lesters will be able to return time and again. I am also hoping that as a flow on from the 'Bringing Them Home Report' individuals will not only be supported in going back to family, but families will be supported in returning to country.

As we do return, we begin to understand how family, land and language are intertwined. Now when I go out bush the majority of grandmothers speak only in traditional language. Even though many of them can speak perfect English they are now at such a point in their lives that they refuse to. They know that if they don't keep their language alive then the meanings of our land and families will be lost. They are determined to show their children and their grandchildren the value of our words and phrases. In the cities, our use of language is changing too. We speak a Creole with English as its basis mixed with elements of our ancestral languages which we are relearning. We struggle with pronunciations, and we watch our children learn more easily than we do, but we are proud to be part of the process of reclamation. Just as we are remaking connections with family and with land, Indigenous peoples around Australia are reclaiming with pride the languages that once we were forbidden to speak.

As Aboriginal people we are bringing the past into the present. One of the saving graces of the Aboriginal community is that we live through extended families. Even if we have lost our biological parents, and this is so very common, there is usually another mother or father that can be found along the way. According to tradition, your father's brothers were your fathers, and your mother's sisters were your mothers. My biological mother is non-Aboriginal and has lived overseas for the last 25 years. We maintain our relationship in the best ways we can, and email is now a blessing, but I felt a very strong need to have an Aboriginal mother and now have a range of them. Some are from within our family group while others are from different clans. We have claimed each other through work that we have done together. One of my Aboriginal mothers, who is of particular significance to me, is not only a gorgeous woman but she was also in the group of six children when my father was taken from the lands. She has a strong connection to my father and some understanding of where I come from. Her presence in my life links my past to my future.

Together we are re-shaping family. We are bringing old ways into the present so that those in the future can live differently. My youngest child, Maya, will always know the land from which our people come. She will always know their stories. When she was born we had the dirt, the Munta, from our country placed in a piti – a wooden carved dish. My sister and my Aunty held our new born and lowered her feet into it so that our country would be the first country that she walked upon. This ritual is now being taken up by others. My nephew on his birth in Sweden was put into Munta from our country, and recently when a Ngarrindjeri baby was born on Kaurna land here in Adelaide, the same ritual unfolded. His feet were placed in Munda from their country. Rituals like these are bringing old ways and new ways together. They give new meaning and significance to our lives and histories. There is so much that can be done to make the lives of our children different from those of our parents.

The key to why I live my life in the ways that I do is my father. As I mentioned earlier, he died when I was 16, and the last time I saw him I was 13. My reason for tracing family is to take him back to what he was taken from. The impact of the missionary system separated him from his people and country. In those days a thousand mile was a thousand mile. That's how far he was taken away. In some missions people were flogged if they spoke their language, flogged if they ate bush tucker. Everything would have reinforced to my father that he came from something that was wrong and all those mixed messages would have been enough to drive anyone crazy.

When I try to think of what my dad would be saying about my attempts to reconnect with our people's history, I think he'd be saying 'Yeah, that's Jane, she's a Lester, a battler'. My father was a very stubborn character. He was also a very violent man - never in a physical sense towards me but physical violence always has an emotional impact regardless if you are on the end of it or not. The last thing my father ever said to me, when I was thirteen, was 'You'll never get anywhere because everyone will always know that you've got black blood.' My response to him was 'I'm going to prove you wrong'.

I was all of 13 years of age standing up to this man. And I think that's what this is all about for me. My mission and purpose has been to bring back a pride to being an Aboriginal person. My father at that time had gone on another binge with his drinking and so I also said to him, 'I am not going to hang around and watch you die.' I was thirteen and never went back. Within weeks I travelled interstate and overseas with my other family. Within three years he had died.

He had lived a life constrained by the elements of time and policy as to who he could be. If he wanted to be a part of this society, there were so few choices available. He had to make the best of the options he was given and in many ways he used these options really well. He was a truck driver and was pulling in a very decent wage for the time. We were seen as no-hoper blackfellas and yet he was pulling in a better wage than half the whitefellas who lived around us.

One of the most significant moments in this whole process of reclaiming family and country occurred quite recently. When I was last out bush I found out that my dad had gone back to country before dying. I had never known this and yet he did it at least twice. To know this means so much to met. He hadn't turned his back on his people, he'd gone to look for them, to look for his father, to look for his mother, to look for his people and his land. I don't know what he found when he went back, but I have continued his search and I have found his people. I have found his land. I have found his father.

And in the process I have found a pride in being an Aboriginal person that once I could not have imagined. I am Jane Lester a Yankunytjatjara/ Antakarinya woman. Our culture is the oldest living culture on earth.

And my father's mother? My grandmother, to whom I dedicate this chapter, what would she think of our efforts? I hope that she'd be pleased that we are coming to find her, to care for her and to care for her memory. We will continue to travel on the wings of the crow and no doubt we will meet each other soon.

Note

This chapter is based on a keynote address that Jane is to give at the Dulwich Centre Publications' international narrative therapy and work conference in Feburary, 2001.

10

Listening to our people's stories of survival

By

Barbara Wingard

Much of our work as Aboriginal Health Workers involves listening to people's stories. To do this well requires skills such as patience not to interrupt, not to break up people's rhythm. If somebody wants to tell me a story then I find I have to be quiet, a little silent, in order to really listen to them. My quietness means that they can collect their thoughts and get themselves on a roll.

Listening involves other skills too. Sometimes when people tell their stories they can become anxious because they want to tell you about their whole life. This can mean the small details get lost, but the small details are sometimes the most important. Listening for small details can be quite hard work. At times I ask people to reflect on something that they have spoken about - just to make that story a little bit richer. Or sometimes I ask them to reflect on a particular event, but this has to be done in a respectful way. I have to take care that I am not going to interrupt their flow.

Perhaps the most important skill involves what we are listening for. Many of us Aboriginal people have been knocked so many times that we often don't think very well of ourselves. That's where a particular kind of listening comes in. We are listening for our people's abilities and knowledges and skills. We're trying to find ways to acknowledge one another and to see the abilities that people have but may not know they have. Without putting people on pedestals, we are finding ways of acknowledging each others' stories of survival.

This is a particular way of listening to people's stories. It is listening for the ways in which people have got through difficult times. It is listening for their special skills or special relationships that have helped them. If we can get people to talk about these things, often life becomes a little easier to live. Let me give an example.

I remember an old lady that I used to visit quite often. She had a large family and they were facing many different problems. There were lots of people living in this particular household and nobody seemed to be listening to her. We both used to enjoy having a chat with each other. I loved listening to her. She used to tell me stories of the ways in which she used to look after all her children. She was determined that the welfare would not get their hands on her kids and so she would catch rabbits and fish to support her family. She had been the main provider in the house for many years and she was very proud of this. I used to wonder if anyone in the family ever used to acknowledge this. She used to love telling me all the different things that she used to do to keep her children fed and to keep the welfare away from them. How she survived really fascinated me. That was what I was listening for, those stories of survival, her skills. I was a witness to these stories and our conversations together would acknowledge those stories of the past. I don't think her family meant to ignore these stories, everybody was simply too busy with their day-to-day lives, but she had such beautiful stories to tell if only someone would listen. She is still very precious to me, although she has been gone a long time.

The skills that she had were remarkable and yet they were not being recognised. This is true in many of our people's lives. That is our role in many ways, to listen for the beautiful stories, to recognise people's skills, to let people re-visit the times in their lives when they have demonstrated those skills. When we're listening for people's skills and their stories of survival, the conversations that take place can be very beautiful.

Gatherings and listening groups

Usually in counselling situations I am listening on my own, but on the gatherings we have held we listen as a team (Aboriginal Health Council of South Australia, 1995). I will just talk about one of these gatherings here that took place in northern NSW. In this gathering three large families came together over a week to try to find ways of healing from the deaths of a number of children.

A key aspect of gatherings like this one is the consultation process that takes place beforehand. Many conversations happen before the gathering and considerable planning takes place. From these consultations with the community a program is developed which contains a number of themes which people have said they wish to talk about. These themes shape what happens on that gathering itself and so it is very important that they come from the community itself.

The listening team, which up until now has been made up of both Aboriginal and non-Aboriginal workers, meets beforehand to make sure that everyone knows each other well. The fact that the listening team members are very close to each other and respect each other is very important.

During the gathering itself the family members move into a number of small circles to discuss each of the themes one at a time. While they are talking to each other some members of the listening team are listening to each group's conversations. They occasionally ask a question or two and they often take some notes if the family members say that this is okay. The listening team members are listening for the stories of survival and the skills and relationships that have helped family members get through hard times. After the family members have finished discussing the theme, all the groups come together into a bigger circle and the listening team sits in the middle.

The listening team members then offer some reflections to each other about what they have heard. The family members all listen in as we re-tell the things that family members said in the small groups. We especially focus on re-telling the stories about people's skills and knowledges and what it meant for us to hear those stories. This means that the family members hear back the things that they were saying in a positive and empowering way. It is like we are acting as an audience to their stories and then we are playing their stories back to them.

When the team has finished, everyone comes together in one large circle to talk about what the process had been like. Listening teams can be a way of honouring what people are saying about their lives. It is important that as members of the listening team we are listening for and then re-telling the positive stories. We reflect on what the families members have said and we always remember that the family members are the experts on their own lives. We are not making judgements on what the families talked about. We are simply re-telling the stories of survival and the stories of skills. We also reflect on what it was like for us to listen to these stories.

It is hard to describe how powerful it can be for people to hear back the stories of their lives in these ways. We are just telling and re-telling stories, but it can make a real difference to people's lives. At the gathering in NSW one person said that watching the listening team was like watching a video of their own lives, and it was the best video they had ever seen! They said they felt like rewinding it and watching it again and again. One of the reasons why it is experienced like this is because the listening team members are listening for empowering stories to reflect back. Great care is taken in how the listening team reflects on people's stories.

As Aboriginal health workers, our role as listeners is really important. We are the audience to people's stories. If we can listen to people's stories, and especially if we can listen for their skills and abilities and acknowledge them in some way, then this can make a real difference to our people's lives. It makes a difference to my life too. I love listening to people's stories.

Reference

Aboriginal Health Council of South Australia, 1995:
     Reclaiming Our Stories, Reclaiming Our Lives.' *Dulwich Centre Newsletter*, 1.

What about the voices that are so often unheard?
What about young workers?

A lot of our people don't get the opportunity for their voices to be heard.
Even amongst Aboriginal Health Workers there are many whom remain
quiet while the voices of the confident take over. This is especially true in
relation to our young people. I am very aware of young people when they
come into the workforce. Everything is so new to them that they are often
afraid to use their voices. They are frightened that they will say the
wrong thing, frightened that they will be shamed if they make mistakes. I
experienced this in my early days at work too, so I am aware of those quiet
people. I am aware that after a meeting some of those who have not
spoken will not feel very good about themselves. They will feel bad that
they did not speak. I used to get quite angry with myself over this.

Sometimes it is respect that gets in the way. Young people feel it is
so important to have respect for older workers, and this is very important,
that they find it very hard to disagree, or to question, or to even have an
opinion, because this can seem to be disrespectful. But respect is a two-
way process. I am interested in how we as elders can acknowledge our
young ones, encourage them to have a point of view, and make it possible
for us to be able to agree to disagree. If we can't agree to disagree then
we are not going to hear young people's voices.

If we can create the possibility for those who are quiet to say
something, if we can find ways to encourage them, then they will feel
really good about themselves. More importantly, we will be able to hear
their ideas. The quiet among us are very skilful and knowledgeable. We
need to hear their voices and opinions.

I am very interested in how we can support young workers and
make it possible for them to develop their own ways of working. This has
been a large part of my work over the last few years. I have great faith in
our young people. They are our future. We need to bring them with us in
this work, and we need to find ways that their voices can be heard.

11

Understanding Homelessness:
An Indigenous Australian Perspective

by

Jane Lester [1]

Trying to understand homelessness from an Aboriginal perspective can be pretty complex. The histories of this country need to be considered. Generations of Aboriginal people have been taken from their lands and taken from their homes - made homeless. As I discussed earlier, my father was stolen. He was part of the Stolen Generation as were his forty or so first cousins.

When we were born, as members of the next generation, we still weren't citizens in this country. Welfare, or the Department, anyone had the right to just walk in and take us away. Our parents didn't have the right to say no. They could say it, but it wasn't heard. In so many ways our people have been taken from their homes and from their land.

The Stolen Generation has had so many effects on Aboriginal people. So many of the struggles that current Indigenous people have are linked to these histories, and our need to come home.

Over recent years, many Aboriginal people have been remaking connections, reclaiming and remaking home. In the process we hear and reconnect with many stories of land, language, culture, and family. We also get to hear about different ways of living, different ways of relating to home. My grandparents, for what we know, did not have a house as such. All I know is that they got around out bush on camels and old drays. I don't know how they did it with the heat and the rains in Central Australia! But they had their ways and they were at home with them. With the coming of the white system, there was a powerful impact. What were believed to be 'pagan' ways were crushed and what were believed to be the 'right' ways to live were imposed. Aboriginal ways have been seen by Europeans as 'barbaric' since the first contact. This includes the ways in which Aboriginal people related to the land, to housing and to home. My grandparents may not have had a house but they lived with a rich sense of home, connected to land and family.

Responses to Indigenous homelessness

Now policy makers look at Aboriginal people who are living out on the streets and make all sorts of assumptions. Here in Adelaide there has been a long-time push to remove Aboriginal people from sitting out in Victoria Square - which is a park in the centre of the city. It is assumed that these people are homeless. Perhaps there may be ways in which these people could be offered assistance with their lives and the ways they are addressing their histories. However, Victoria Square has always been a meeting place for Aboriginal people. It is a meeting place from a long way back. This is why Aboriginal people spend their days there. And this is why it is so inappropriate for policy makers to try to drive these people away. Some of the Aboriginal people who frequent Victoria Square have homes to go to but they choose to spend some of their time in the Square. We can't make assumptions about the meanings for Aboriginal people of being without a house. Some people living without houses may have a strong sense of home, dignity and connectedness.

This doesn't mean we shouldn't be taking action and finding ways to assist Aboriginal people who need housing. The effects of the Stolen Generation and the histories of this country mean that many Aboriginal people are struggling with substance abuse and other issues. Many Aboriginal people are struggling with finding a home. When Indigenous people do need assistance, histories must be considered. In an Aboriginal context, when different members in the extended family have been seen not to cope, it is far more likely that they'll be passed on to others in the family rather than passed onto the welfare because of the damage that welfare has done to Aboriginal people. For Aboriginal people who are struggling with homelessness, finding ways for them remake connections with culture, land and family may be important first steps.

Beyond welfare

Some of my nieces and nephews have done something like 40 placements in foster care. One placement lasted six hours. The impact that this has on young children's lives is significant. I remember driving along with my nephew when he was about four years old and noticing that he was spotting welfare cars. Instead of spotting Volkswagens which was a game played at the time, he was spotting welfare cars. The reality of many Aboriginal children's lives is that welfare and the police seem very close.

Over the years, the Aboriginal Child Care Agency has questioned why so many Aboriginal children were going into the welfare system. Recently they have ensured that Aboriginal children cannot be adopted in South Australia. Now a certain code of practice applies when Aboriginal children come into the system of family services. Aboriginal representatives need to be involved and appropriate members of the extended family need to be discovered before any formal placement is decided. It is recognised now that families must have input into what is going on for Aboriginal children.

For one of my nieces, we knew that her foster placement was eventually going to break down, therefore we asked the family that we be contacted immediately should this transpire so that my niece didn't have to go through the process of living with yet another family that was unknown to her.

For Aboriginal children there is a real irony of being wards of the state. Having the Minister see himself as your father is a little complex when you are Aboriginal, given the histories of this country! We have to find appropriate ways in which Aboriginal families and communities can be supported in caring for family members who are struggling.

Gradually, more and more Aboriginal people are coming home to their families, their culture and their land. As we do so, we will need to find ways of addressing issues of homelessness that do justice to the complexities of our history and that also honour Indigenous ways or relating to land, to housing and to home.

Note

1.   This chapter was adapted from an interview published in the Dulwich Centre Journal 1999 No. 3

Part 2

Working together towards culturally appropriate services

Introduction

by

Barbara Wingard

As mentioned in previous chapters, many things get in the way of Aboriginal people accessing mainstream health services. There are barriers due to history and there are barriers caused by current policies and practices that exclude Aboriginal understandings and ways of living. It is a continual challenge for many Aboriginal Health Workers to work with others to develop culturally appropriate services and practices.

In this section we have included two documents from research projects which focus on the question 'what would culturally appropriate services look like?'. Chapter 12, 'Towards culturally appropriate services' was the result of research that took place in 1995 in the Adelaide area into the cultural sensitivity, appropriateness and accessibility of mainstream health services. This research was commissioned by the Aboriginal Health Council of South Australia following on from the gathering that was held at Camp Coorong for families who had lost a family member through a death in custody. Chapter 13, 'Working together' consists of extracts from research conducted in 2000 in the Hills Mallee Southern Region of South Australia.

Both projects involved interviewing Aboriginal and non-Aboriginal workers about their experiences and thoughts in relation to cultural appropriateness. These interviews involved listening to people's stories and documenting them in their own words. A lot of care needed to be taken in this process. The interviews needed to be carried out in respectful ways so that it was acknowledged that the stories people were telling were precious. Finding ways of documenting these stories seems very important because otherwise people do not get to hear of the great ideas and work that people are coming up with.

Placed together, these two documents describe some of the key issues that we need to be thinking through in relation to developing culturally appropriate services for Aboriginal people. It was interesting to me to see how in the five years since the first study there have been considerable changes in understanding. The The 'Working Together' document in chapter 12, seems more positive and hopeful than the research described in chapter13. There seem to be many more connections between what the Indigenous people and the non-Indigenous people are saying now, than they were five years ago. There seems to be more awareness and understanding these days. Then again, this could also be because the 'Working Together' project took place in a regional area, where there are a range of Aboriginal workers, rather than a metropolitan context where some services have no Aboriginal workers and few Aboriginal clients.

What was clear in all of the interviews is that generally speaking people are willing to learn and wanting to know how to make their services more accessible. People don't want to make mistakes. What's also clear is that the ways in which health and mental health services are run are going to need to change in a variety of ways if Aboriginal people's understandings are going to be respected. Things have changed a lot since I began working and we need to go on with these changes. Rather than being fearful of change why not embrace it? As Aboriginal people we have had to deal with so many changes in the past two hundred years.

We hope that by publishing these two documents here Aboriginal Health Workers may be able to use them to create further discussion and change. Perhaps the chapter could be photocopied and handed out to others in the workplace. This maybe easier for other Aboriginal Health Workers rather than having to raise issues in isolation.

In the coming year we plan on creating another document, one which includes the voices of community members with their ideas about services. The voices of community members are not often heard when it comes to developing services and so this will be a chance for their views to be respected.

We have come to realise that the process of doing these interviews and documenting these stories also creates change and brings about a different sort of awareness. When people see their words in print, alongside the stories of other people, they feel joined in some way, and taken seriously. The journey towards culturally appropriate services is going to be a long one. It seems important to trace our steps along the way.

12

Towards culturally appropriate services[1]

There are serious questions about the ability of mainstream services to respond, in culturally sensitive and appropriate ways, to the broad range of issues facing Aboriginal people. This chapter relates the findings of a study of the cultural sensitivity, appropriateness and accessibility of mainstream health services. The research involved interviewing mainstream agencies that provide social and mental health services to determine:

- the extent to which Aboriginal people used their service
- whether their service employed culturally appropriate practices
- any ideas they might have about what would make their services more culturally appropriate and accessible to the needs of Aboriginal people.

This report presents the findings of this research project.

Representatives from Aboriginal organisations were interviewed to seek their opinions on these issues and to gain a clear picture from the community of what they felt was important. We also interviewed people from different communities specifically to hear and document their personal stories of how mainstream services had impacted upon their lives. This included questions about what they saw as important features of an agency, and what made them feel comfortable and encouraged to use a particular service.

In total, over 100 people, representing more than 45 different agencies, both Aboriginal and non-Aboriginal, were interviewed during a ten week period. The interviews were conducted by two teams, made up wherever possible of an Aboriginal and non-Aboriginal counsellor. While the majority of the interviews took place within the Adelaide metropolitan area, some were also conducted at Murray Bridge, Ceduna, Pt Augusta and Coober Pedy.

A broad cross-section of the mental and social health services in South Australia were represented in the interview sample of mainstream services, including prisons, hospitals, community health centres, agencies that dealt with psychiatric and mental illness, social and welfare issues, employment, schools, police, community centres and public utilities.

While most of the people interviewed stated clearly that they were not acting as formal representatives of their specific agencies, but rather, that they were giving accounts of their own personal experiences and insights, these experiences of course have come from working within an agency setting. However, for these reasons, neither agencies nor individuals will be referred to by name.

This document does not claim to be a definitive report on the mental and social health needs of the Aboriginal community. It represents a brief overview of a selection of agencies in South Australia, and there were many important services that we were unable to approach due to time constraints. However, irrespective of the agencies interviewed, there were consistent themes that emerged.

Overview of findings

It was clear that Aboriginal people are not accessing mainstream services and that there is a great and urgent need for culturally appropriate services.

During the interviews a number of different perceptions of the problem were found among mainstream services.

1) Some recognised that there is a major problem, openly admitted that they don't know what to do about it, and said that they would welcome advice and direction as well as support and assistance.

> *There was an attempt some time back to get together with a variety of agencies serving this area, Aboriginal organisations and local Aboriginal representatives, to address Aboriginal issues. We held a few meetings at the main office, but over time, all the Aboriginal people stopped coming. Seems to be a common problem ... They are now employing a research officer to find out why.* (non-Aboriginal worker in a mental health agency)

2) Some services clearly had not given any thought to the issues involved, did not recognise that there is a problem, and did not believe that they have any responsibility to review their practices and provision of services. Some clearly felt that they had done all that could be expected of them, and that it was Aboriginal people's fault that their efforts had not been successful. The view that Aboriginal people already get "more than their fair share" of state support was also put forward on more than one occasion.

This was particularly clear in the area of employment policies regarding Aboriginal people. Concepts of "equal opportunity" were understood as relieving services of needing to take any positive action.

> *Q: In this building, where there appears to be more than one hundred staff, would you have any Aboriginal employees?*
>
> *A: No.*
>
> *Q: Are you aware of having employed Aboriginal people in the past?*
>
> *A: No. I'm not aware of there having been Aboriginal people here, and because of our equal opportunity policy, there are no specific future plans to positively discriminate in favour of Aboriginal applicants.* (personnel officer in major government utility)

3) Aboriginal workers reported that mainstream agencies often believe that the existence of Aboriginal services means that they don't have to take any responsibility for Aboriginal people at all.

> *The local hospital always rings me when there's an Aboriginal patient about*

to leave. They want me to organise their transport home. I say to them, "what do you do for other patients?" and they say, "we ring a taxi" and I say, "why can't you do the same?" They don't seem to realise that I've got other things that I have to be doing, that are more urgent than ferrying someone home from the hospital. (Aboriginal health worker)

We often get phone calls late on a Friday afternoon from the hospital asking us to take charge of an Aboriginal patient whom they are about to discharge. They say the person's got nowhere to go for the weekend, and we say they should have planned long before discharge time what they were going to do.

They expect because we are an Aboriginal agency, that we should pick up the tab. They need to assume the same duty of care for Aboriginal patients that they do for any other patients. (non-Aboriginal health worker)

4) Aboriginal and non-Aboriginal workers employed in Aboriginal organisations, and in Aboriginal units within mainstream services, were generally clear about what needs to be done, and held similar views. Their major recommendations included:

(a) A clear recognition, on the part of government and mainstream services of the seriousness of the existing problem, and the urgency of taking action.

(b)The central need for Aboriginal self-determination and autonomy in the development and provision of services to Aboriginal people.

(c) Recognition that the health and service needs of Aboriginal people cannot be separated from the wider context of injustice that Aboriginal experience as part of their every day lives, and the need to address this wider context of injustice.

(d) Increased willingness on the part of mainstream services to learn from and take direction from Aboriginal people, as well as accepting support and assistance from Aboriginal people, so that their services can be as culturally appropriate and as accessible as possible.

Mainstream services need to question their practices because what's currently available is not working. They need to work collaboratively with Aboriginal people. We need to have Aboriginal people working in mainstream organisations. Next year, I hope to have 3 people stand for local council elections. They need to be in positions of influence, have an active say within the wider community. (Aboriginal activist and community worker)

(e) A recognition, on the part of mainstream services, that the existence of independent Aboriginal services does not relieve them of responsibility for addressing these issues. Mainstream services have a responsibility to provide appropriate services to the whole community, including to Aboriginal people.

We need autonomous Aboriginal agencies to address Aboriginal issues. The existing agencies do not address Aboriginal issues and do not understand the issues of Aboriginal people. Aboriginal people need self-determination and autonomous services, yet also need to know how to address and access mainstream services. (Aboriginal director of an Aboriginal agency)

Aboriginal people need their own autonomous services and they need to be able to utilise mainstream services. There is no way the latter can meet the needs of the Aboriginal community as a service like an Aboriginal medical service can, however, mainstream services should make themselves more accessible than many currently do. Then Aboriginal people have the choice to decide, they have the power in their own lives, their own decision-making. (non-Aboriginal community health nurse)

Why are Aboriginal people not accessing mainstream services?

General context of injustice

Mainstream services have historically been implicated in the oppression of Aboriginal people. The continued existence of injustices operates as a barrier to Aboriginal people's willingness to use mainstream services. There is a feeling that these services are either not intended for their use, or actively hostile to their needs. A major example of this is in the area of child and family "welfare" services, which in Aboriginal eyes, are still implicated in the forced removal of children. This makes many Aboriginal people extremely reluctant to become involved with such services.

The main cause for "dysfunction" in the Aboriginal family and society goes back to the forced removal policy of children from their families. The assimilationist policy is still alive today. We still have social workers who say that Aboriginal people cannot take care of their children. Or they say, "This kid's skin is too pale to place him/her with an Aboriginal family."

In one particular case, there was a young child at a major hospital here in Adelaide, who had come down for treatment. The nurse on the ward "fell in love" with this little black baby. With the assistance of a social work friend, who knew the relevant people to contact, the nurse was able to take the baby home, and to begin adoption proceedings, on the grounds that the baby still required medical attention which was assumed that the baby's family could not properly administer. The network of "professionals" supported the adoption. Despite the issue of removal of an Aboriginal child from his/her biological family, and removing the child from his/her culture, custody was eventually granted to the non-Aboriginal family. No effort was made to contact the extended family members for placement of this child.

An Aboriginal agency took this case to court, but did not have the finances to act quickly following such legal actions and so, by the time this case was presented in court, it was more than a year since the adoption and the child had bonded to the new family. The court stated that it would have been "unfair to remove the child now." This is not an isolated event - there have been many black babies adopted by nursing staff under such situations which have been upheld by the state. (Aboriginal director of an Aboriginal agency)

Access

When Aboriginal people do want to make use of existing services, they often report a great deal of difficulty actually getting to them. The reasons given were:

1) Poverty and unemployment severely reduce Aboriginal people's ability to travel in order to access services, and are a major reason for their need for services. Many Aboriginal people have no car of their own and no access to public transport. There is often no telephone easily accessible. Aboriginal people made it clear that they want jobs, to have a sense of purpose in their lives, to have

pride and a sense of achievement, and to provide role models for their children.

When you give an Aboriginal person a job you're uplifting their whole health status. (Aboriginal health worker)

The facts are that 49% of the Aboriginal population is unemployed. In Salisbury, in one family, there were 5 people unemployed. These people never have the chance to get off the dole. There are generations of people out of work. (Aboriginal director of a community centre)

Aboriginal people interviewed identified the range of employment services currently available as inappropriate and inaccessible to Aboriginal people, due to the services' lack of cultural awareness. This non-utilisation was more likely to be interpreted by non-Aboriginal people in the light of racist stereotypes about Aboriginal unwillingness to work, rather than as evidence of the need for action on the part of mainstream services.

An Aboriginal man from a remote community was released from gaol, and applied for unemployment benefits. When he was asked if he would be looking for work when he returned to his community, he replied "no" - thus failing the "work test". He was not advised that his answer made him ineligible for benefits. His understanding of English was limited and he was partly blind. His answer had come from his knowledge that there was no work on his community to look for. A system that required him to say he was looking for work, despite the fact that everyone, including the interviewing officer, knew that there was no work on remote communities, was incomprehensible to this man. When he returned to his community he waited for his cheque for nearly two months before talking to me. When I worked out what had happened, I contacted Social Security, explained the situation, and asked for him to be back-paid. He had, I asserted, been the victim of culturally inappropriate behaviour on the part of the interviewing staff member. Social Security agreed to reinstate his benefits, but refused to back-pay him - causing him and his family a great deal of financial hardship. (non-Aboriginal community worker)

2) Many Aboriginal people live in areas that are a long way from any mainstream services and their communities do not have sufficient funding to establish their own.

3) Mainstream services are often reluctant to provide outreach services - Aboriginal people are expected to come to them, rather than the services be taken to Aboriginal people.

Cultural Differences

There are important differences between Aboriginal and non-Aboriginal ways of being, and different meanings are often given to concepts central to the provision of services. In the context of injustice and powerlessness, non-Aboriginal meanings are often imposed on Aboriginal people. This makes access difficult because the very understandings and cultural meanings that inform service provision are alien or hostile to Aboriginal people. Examples of areas where differences in meaning are important include:

Health

Aboriginal people made it clear that, for them, "health" is a collective, not individual, concept. It encompasses the well-being of the wider family members, issues of loss and grief, and socio-economic factors like housing, employment, and education.

> *"Health" to an Aboriginal person - they don't see it as a separate issue from all the other things that are happening in their lives. There are different issues for Aboriginal people than what non-Aboriginal people think - its issues to do with daily living. Mainstream services compartmentalise issues - they need to deal with us as a family.* (Aboriginal health worker)

Family

"Family" is of central importance in Aboriginal people's lives, and it can have a quite different meaning than in non-Aboriginal society.

> *Concepts of child-parent relationships amongst Aboriginal people are different to that currently held in non-Aboriginal groups. Children float around amongst the whole family network, among the aunties, grandmothers, cousins, and get cared for much more on a collective basis. They are well looked after, and it can be a very good thing to share the parenting, especially if the*

mother's ill or distressed. The kids seem pretty happy about it. There is a strong sense of kin, of extended family networks, duty and responsibilities. (non-Aboriginal priest and director of an Aboriginal community service)

My understanding is that 'health' is viewed socially, that 'health' hinges upon the unity and wholeness, well-being of the whole family. So, if a member of the family is incarcerated or forcibly removed, or in hospital, so that they are removed from the family unit, then the very emotional/psychological and spiritual foundations of the family are eroded away. It's then that an individual might recognise that they are ill or not feeling well. Wellness hinges upon the unity of the whole family. (non-Aboriginal community health nurse)

Shame

Non-Aboriginal people interviewed reported some difficulty understanding the concept of shame, but recognised that it impacts powerfully upon Aboriginal people's lives. It was described as including a range of emotions, such as embarrassment, disgrace and humiliation. The current practices of mainstream services are often experienced by Aboriginal people as shaming, providing a strong barrier to their ability to utilise these services, or to participate more fully in the wider society.

I've got a photo of myself and my sister ... we were little tackers, but our heads were down ... but that's the way we were brought up, you never looked at older people much... a lot of it had to do with respect for our elderly ... The difficulty I first had, I was 29 when I first started to work ... I would walk down the street, and people would look at me, and I would automatically put my head down ...

We are a people of few words and I think that's where there are a few difficulties in learning and to be trained ... and be like anybody else, this fear of, "oh, I'm gonna say it the wrong way ... I'm gonna say it back-to-front"... the fear of I'm not gonna be able to say it properly in front of white people". And believe me, it's terrible.

I know of a young Aboriginal woman who has recently started work ... in a mainstream environment, she found it really scary ... having to use phones, talk in front of other people, especially white people, she is threatened by the building and the way things are organised around her. It's a shame job for her. (Aboriginal health worker)

Grief and Loss

Grief and loss are a constant presence in Aboriginal people's lives, in a way that is usually incomprehensible to most non-Aboriginal people. This grief and loss stems from a variety of factors, including the long history of dispossession and genocide, forced removal of children, deaths in custody, ill-health, and suicide. Many of the people dying are young, leading to a fear for the very future of their community. The lack of awareness of these losses, on the part of the wider community, intensifies the sense of injustice and powerlessness experienced by many Aboriginal people in the face of these losses.

> *I've been here a few years now. When I first came, I made myself and the bus available to take community members to funerals, we'd go out to Pt. Pearce and Pt. Macleay ... In my years here, I've seen a lot of people die. Young people, especially people aged between 15 and 23 years ... 4 out of every 6 deaths are people under the age of 35 years. Sometimes, there are a couple of funerals a week. There's one family that I know that have lost 3 members in the last 18 months. People live in a cycle of grief, they no sooner have one death in the family, when another one occurs. They never get an adequate chance to mourn for their family member when there's another death. Aboriginal people are in a state of being stunned, their family members die so young, and so frequently. And the lack of support services is incredible. These people need more than just a straight-out G.P. health service, they need in-depth family counselling to begin to address these issues of pain and loss and grief.*
> (non-Aboriginal priest and director of an Aboriginal community service)

> *They ask me to mark on a diagram where the pain is, this side, or that. "It's all over" I'd say. They don't understand that part of it is bereavement pain.*
> (Aboriginal elder)

> *I deal with family and health problems together. I have a recognition that losses need to be acknowledged ... death in families, particularly many deaths, leads to alcohol abuse and other forms of abuse and distress, violence, street kids. The impact has a chain reaction. This is not recognised within the wider community generally, how loss and fear and ill-health all impact upon the health of the family and the individual.* (non-Aboriginal community health nurse)

Lack of understanding of Aboriginal ways and meanings

Lack of understanding of Aboriginal ways and meanings, including those listed above, results in inappropriate, insensitive and disrespectful practices that form a powerful barrier to Aboriginal people's ability and willingness to utilise mainstream services.

> *The bulk of Aboriginal people who are admitted to psychiatric institutions do not come of their own volition ... some people are acting out in culturally-appropriate ways, and we need to know, to decide whether Western interventions are appropriate.* (non-Aboriginal psychiatrist in a major psychiatric institution)

One Aboriginal man told a story which illustrates the effects of mainstream services not understanding, and not respecting different meanings and practices in Aboriginal families.

> *This man's wife was in hospital a long way from home, and in order to visit her he had to leave his two young children at home in the care of his 14 year old son. The fourteen year old was an excellent hunter, and was quite able to look after the children and provide food as well. He had two very well trained dogs to help him in this task. As well, the wider family were keeping an eye on them. The local welfare services heard that the children were "not being looked after" and came to take the children into "care". The older boy ordered the dogs to chase them away, and they did not return.*

Lack of Recognition of the diversity of Aboriginal people and communities

> *If you're in a room with a heap of white people, they expect you to be up on all the issues, like Mabo, and because you're Nunga, you know, "Give me your views!" and that's the awkward bit, they expect you to speak for all Nungas. And, you know, that's not an easy thing to do ... I often say to people, I don't want to speak on behalf of all Nungas, this is my personal view.* (Aboriginal health worker)

> *An old Aboriginal man from a remote community was sent down to Adelaide*

with kidney failure. He spoke virtually no English, and the nursing staff got hold of a list of 'Aboriginal" words, stuck them up on the wall and tried to communicate with him. He became more and more uncooperative and was regarded as one of the most "difficult" patients in the hospital. It was not until the non-Aboriginal advisor from his community came down to visit him that the hospital discovered they were using the wrong language entirely. No effort had been made, when he arrived, to find out where he was from and what language he spoke. (non-Aboriginal community worker)

Lack of consultation with Aboriginal people

Lack of consultation with Aboriginal people has historically been a major reason for the absence of appropriate service provision, even where goodwill existed. Aboriginal people and some non-Aboriginal workers employed in Aboriginal services emphasised that non-Aboriginal people must not presume to understand the premises from which Aboriginal people operate. They stressed that consultation is the only way that inappropriate and disrespectful practices can be avoided.

Lack of consultation with the Aboriginal community and individuals leads to a sense of powerlessness, confirms Aboriginal invisibility in wider society and underscores a sense of worthlessness. Mainstream agencies are seen as paternalistic and disrespectful by Aboriginal people for not seeking their involvement in decisions that affect them.

I was working on a community, and one of the older men approached me and asked if I'd track down his brother, in Adelaide. Apparently he'd gone to have some minor operation, like having his in-grown toe-nails seen to, something like that, and he hadn't come back. I was told he might be at this particular place, as that was the last place that they'd heard of him.

I was able to track this old man down. He was staying in a residential-care type centre where Aboriginal people could go to recuperate before returning to their lands and families. They're only meant to stay a few weeks.

He could speak English, not very well, and it sounded a bit garbled, but he could speak. But he's been left alone by the staff because they thought that he couldn't, and 'cause, he was old, and black, and gnarled. When I spoke with him and could talk a bit of his language, he told me that he was "sick, sorry, sad and upset". I asked him how long he'd been there. "Seven years". I asked him how this had happened, why he hadn't been sent home long ago, why the staff hadn't contacted his family to get him? He told me, "they didn't think to ask". And he assumed they knew his situation, and that if they were keeping him there, that there must be some reason. I asked him if he wanted to go home and was able to arrange it. (non-Aboriginal community worker)

Absence of links with the Aboriginal community

Absence of links with the Aboriginal community means that Aboriginal people are entering an alien or hostile environment when seeking to access services. The very nature of this environment is a barrier to Aboriginal access. Without good links with the Aboriginal community, consultation is itself more difficult, as there are no established and effective means of getting in touch with key people when the need arises. It is extremely difficult to build up trust when there are no on-going links between services and Aboriginal communities, and this leads to little, or no utilisation of services by Aboriginal people. This non-utilisation can have tragic consequences:

I married young. Yeah, ... very shy young girl.... I never went to the doctor's until I was seven months pregnant, because we didn't do that, we didn't go to the doctors unless we were sick ... dreading that first examination that they do ... shame job. I know it's difficult for anybody, but especially with Aboriginal women. I regret it... I share this story with a lot of young girls ... because when I had my baby, they didn't know that I was having twins! On delivery day ... it was a total surprise ... I'll never forget that, they said, there's another one here! But, unfortunately, that little baby only lived for two days. He was a breech baby, and he was hiding behind the other twin. The first twin was getting all the nourishment. This one lived for two days and he died with chest complications and that. And I always regret that I never had the proper check-ups, because it could have made all the difference, you know, if I'd had those examinations. But still, what's happened happened ...nobody knew ... I never blamed the doctors or anyone like that. But it is an example that I use with our young girls now, how important it is to make sure they go and have the checkups. (Aboriginal health worker)

We could paint this whole building the colours of the Aboriginal flag and it still wouldn't attract more Aboriginal people here. It's the links that we have to work on ... between the two communities ... Understanding, working together, respecting difference. (non-Aboriginal community health nurse)

The alien nature of the mainstream service environment

There are a number of ways in which the alien nature of the mainstream service environment is manifested:

1) Attitudes of non-Aboriginal workers

Aboriginal people reported that the attitudes of non-Aboriginal workers in mainstream agencies are often a barrier to Aboriginal utilisation of these services. They talked about the widespread nature of practices such as:

- prying too far into personal details and not knowing when to stop
- using disrespectful language such as "half-caste"
- not asking permission before taking action affecting Aboriginal people
- not ensuring that Aboriginal people understand what is being proposed before going ahead

I asked the nurse on duty if there were any Aboriginal people here, and he said, "There's no blackfellas on this ward". (Aboriginal liaison officer)

This fella, he's got a big family and he takes them to the doctor and he told them why he came. But he feels they are not listening to him. He said, "Oh, they give you pills and you can go home" He said they don't really listen to you. He gets so frustrated with doctors because the doctors are so educated they think they've got all the answers, and no-one else knows, you know. And this is the same with educated people, they think they've got all the answers, and no-one else knows what's wrong with them. And it's the people who are suffering themselves that know. (Aboriginal field officer)

A lot of people will dodge a particular doctor, won't go into see that doctor, they'll wait until the other one's available. At the surgery... this is years ago when my son was born and he had an ear infection, you know, he was complaining and crying about his ear, so I took him there. And the doctor didn't want to touch him, didn't want to look in his ear. I could feel myself getting worked up, riled, you know, and I was thinking to myself, what's wrong, is it because he's black or, you know? It just made me wild so I couldn't be bothered going back there again, and I just went straight to the chemist and bought ear drops.

I'd be asking all my other people, "who's the best doctor"? And you hear other people ... they tell you the best, who does a fairer job and who doesn't. I've always been a bit wary ... and we talk amongst ourselves, too, about doctors and things, and usually to ask for that particular doctor that's got a good reputation. If they are not that really sick, we leave it till the next morning, till the surgery's open and then try and squeeze in with that doctor whom we like. (Aboriginal health worker)

2) Attitudes of non-Aboriginal people using the service

The attitudes and behaviour of non-Aboriginal people using mainstream services was also reported to be a major barrier to Aboriginal people being able to utilise those services.

I did a role play last year about a waiting room, and I was in the role as a "rough lady" with lots of problems, and I used a lot of my own experiences within that lady. And I yelled at all the people, "What are you looking at? What are you staring at?" Because that's what happens to us, they stare at us. And I've taken clients to the doctors and I've heard little kids saying "look at the monkey". And you can just feel it. (Aboriginal health worker)

This agency decided last year to open between Christmas Day and New Year's Eve. Something that we haven't done in the past. The doctor and myself were the two left here to run the place. Word must have got out to the Aboriginal community, because the day after Christmas, I was here and in came one of the women front the local community and asked if I'd see her relatives. I said yes, and the next thing, there were about 18 women and children coming in the door, all laughing and fooling around, because they knew they were the only ones here, they felt relaxed and this woman had told them that we were workers to be trusted. It must have been one of the biggest, and noisiest, and the most relaxed groups of Aboriginal people to have ever used the centre at one time. And they came because they knew that there were unlikely to be other, that is, non-Aboriginal, people here. And also, because someone they trusted had brought them, that's really important, especially for people who don't speak the language. (non-Aboriginal community health nurse)

3) Absence of Aboriginal staff

The absence of Aboriginal faces on the other side of the counter underlines Aboriginal perceptions that they do not belong and are not welcome in these services. The factors limiting Aboriginal employment in these services include:

(a) The qualifications, knowledge and experience of Aboriginal workers are often not recognised or are down-graded. They are often not seen to be "professionals" in their own right, and their work is not valued or recognised by other agency staff, or by the non-Aboriginal community more generally.

'Aboriginal people are second-best" is the general attitude of the community. Academics do not regard our community organisations and workers as being skilled, and academics can be obstructive to community based workers. I have seen judges base decisions to place children with non-Aboriginal families following the advice of middle-class, non-Aboriginal professionals. (Aboriginal director of an Aboriginal agency)

The Aboriginal Health Workers are viewed more as taxi drivers than part of the medical hierarchy. (non-Aboriginal social worker at a major hospital)

Terms and conditions of employment for Aboriginal people are generally inferior compared to other workplace situations. Although Aboriginal people are quite capable, they often haven't had the same education and employment opportunities available to them. Many jobs that are on offer are short-term, maybe 3 or 6 months, with no guarantees of renewal. Makes for an uncertain working environment that people are often not willing to pursue. Of jobs that are of a more permanent nature, there are often no career opportunities, no mobility within the job. Other issues to be looked at include pay, classifications, time off for ceremonies. These are areas that need to be addressed. (non-Aboriginal doctor at a community health centre)

(b) A lack of understanding or an acceptance of responsibility, or at times hostility, on the part of mainstream agencies to the concepts of equal opportunity and affirmative action. There is often little understanding of the special circumstances and experiences of Aboriginal people which may mean that simply treating them "the same as everyone else" contributes to the continued existence of injustice, inequality and exclusion.

The public relations officer of one major service provider said the following:

This organisation operates under Equal Opportunity Legislation, and as such does not treat Aboriginal people any differently from any other group in society, the same as we do not discriminate, either positively or negatively, in any way regarding any other specific service that is provided for Aboriginal people.

We do not have any specific culturally appropriate services for Aboriginal people, as we similarly do not have any for any other groups in society. We have no specific interpreter services available, we just deal with issues as they arise.

We know that Aboriginal people are fairly localised, and that they tend to live within their family groupings, but Aboriginal people are only a small part of our customers. We have no records that indicate whether there are specific problems within specific cultural groups, we have no records to show that there are any particular strategies or services that are required by particular groups within the broader community.

(c) The practice of employing a single Aboriginal worker creates impossible pressures and demands on that worker. Trying to change the culture and practices of a workplace single handed can be a long, lonely battle, and is often very demoralising. A lone Aboriginal worker in an agency can feel isolated, and can feel that their employment was a token gesture. They are often met with alien systems and environment, and can be faced with very large workload.

I was the only Aboriginal worker there, so anything that came up about any Aboriginal people I was called to see. Lots of things the white staff could have done. I was always on the go. And there was no-one there to talk with, no-one to share the load. I thought there's got to be a better way to work. I lasted 6 weeks. (Aboriginal community health worker)

I feel very alone and isolated. The staff are really racist. When I first started I left pamphlets about equal opportunity around, but people either ignored them or tore them up. I don't want to be the "token black"... I feel discriminated against. I felt very timid at first working there, but then I had to start fighting for myself. I encountered a lot of gossip and discrimination. I was told to "stop carrying the flag", told to pull my head in. The staff think that if you are working there you've got to cut the cultural stuff off. But it doesn't work like that – I'm an Aboriginal first and foremost. (Aboriginal liaison officer)

4) Physical Layout

The physical layout of buildings is often experienced by Aboriginal people as alien and intimidating. Agencies need to consult with Aboriginal people in order to make these environments comfortable and accessible for Aboriginal people.

5) Organisation

The way that mainstream services are organised often makes them unresponsive or inappropriate to Aboriginal ways of being and needs. Aboriginal people reported difficulty with the following practices:

- The lack of flexibility with appointment times and having to make appointments at.
- The lack of flexibility over length of consultations.
- The absence of opportunities for home visiting.

These practices reflect a lack of knowledge of the contexts of many Aboriginal people's lives. They may not be able to plan ahead for a visit to town, but simply take the offer of a lift when it arises. Whole families may arrive together, all needing attention, but may be unwilling to come for individual appointments.

What would culturally-appropriate and accessible services look like, and what would make them possible

These recommendations are based upon:

- Practices already operating in a number of organisations.
- Ideas about ideal practices suggested by Aboriginal people and non-Aboriginal people working in the provision of services to the Aboriginal community.

Self-Determination and Autonomy

Both Aboriginal people and non-Aboriginal workers in the area of Aboriginal services clearly see issues of autonomy and self-determination as paramount. The recommendations made included:

- Establishment of, and increased funding for, independent Aboriginal service organisations.
- Establishing self-determining and autonomous units within mainstream agencies, rather than employing a single worker.
- Enshrining the autonomy and independence of Aboriginal organisations in legislation.

I'd give them the money and let them get on with it ... and that goes without any accountability to the dominant culture. (non-Aboriginal manager in a mainstream welfare service.)

Non-Aboriginals working with Aboriginal workers should trust that Aboriginals can rectify their own mistakes and therefore respect the principles of self-determination. (Aboriginal director of an Aboriginal agency)

Non-Aboriginal people should offer to help Aboriginal people e.g. with training, with submission writing and support them in their applications for funding. Aboriginal health bodies and non-Aboriginal organisations should get together at a macro level and begin planning strategies together. Then non-Aboriginal people should withdraw. (Aboriginal director of an Aboriginal service)

> *Let Aboriginal people develop their own strategies for operating both in
> a mainstream service and in a separate service. Aboriginal people need
> their own autonomous services and they need to be able to utilise
> mainstream services. There is no way the latter can meet the needs of the
> Aboriginal community as a service like an Aboriginal medical service
> can, however, mainstream services should make themselves more
> accessible than many currently do. Then Aboriginal people have the
> choice to decide, they have the power in their own lives, their own
> decision-making.* (non-Aboriginal health care nurse)

Aboriginal workers stressed that the existence of autonomous Aboriginal
services does not mean that mainstream services have no responsibility for
Aboriginal people. Mainstream services have a duty to the *whole community*
to act in appropriate, sensitive and respectful ways. This includes the
responsibility to make sure that Aboriginal people are able to access these
services *in practice,* not just in theory.

Consultation

Mainstream services need to develop links with the Aboriginal community and
consult with Aboriginal people and organisations on all matters concerning
Aboriginal people.

> *There is much room for error when dealing with Aboriginal people, whose
> beliefs, understandings and perceptions are so different from non-
> Aboriginals'. Our body movement, eye contact ... is very different. Aboriginal
> people say that non-Aboriginals talk, but don't communicate. So, there's lots of
> room for mistakes when working with Aboriginal people. The key is to be guided
> by them, ask their opinion, say that you don't know what to do, what is
> appropriate. Seek their direction. Mainstream agencies have a history of getting
> it wrong. We need to ask how to get it right. People working in partnership,
> understanding each other's value systems ... this is the way forward. Unless there
> is a basis of understanding we will be unable to overcome all of the problems.
> There is need for consultation and liaison with Aboriginal people at every
> stage.* (non-Aboriginal health worker in an Aboriginal agency)

Just because we are disadvantaged doesn't mean we do not have our own ideas about how we want disadvantage addressed. (Aboriginal director of an Aboriginal service)

All the doctors got together and they wanted to start a reconciliation meeting here. And I walked up to this fella and another bloke and asked them if they wanted to be in the reconciliation meeting with the doctors from town. They just looked at me and said, "Why? They don't listen to me in the surgery ... so why would I have a meeting with them?" I said, "That's the perfect reason to go and to explain it and to talk to them about it and say that they are not listening to you ... explain the situation. Well, they went ahead with their reconciliation meetings. They've come to the end of their time, but they are still going to continue and are organising the next round. Now that's really good. And those two blokes, they went there right throughout it ... they like sitting down ...

Q: And did they find that the doctor was listening to them?

Oh yeah, they wouldn't have been back there if they hadn't ... all talking about things to do, so it's really good. That fella ... he feels free now to go and visit [the doctor] and talk ... have a chat with them... express themselves. Whereas before, the doctors would not give their Aboriginal clients much credence, after the reconciliation meetings, even the doctors sort of realised they need to listen too. (Aboriginal field officer)

For effective consultation to be possible it is crucial for services to develop links with the Aboriginal community. This allows an understanding of who the key people are who should be approached, and it allows services to show respect for and operate within existing community networks.

In an agency like this health centre, key people who provide links with the Aboriginal community are crucial. We had an older Aboriginal woman employed here for a time and she set up meetings here with various people from the community. People like her are very important. They need to advise this service, and we need to listen. (non-Aboriginal community health nurse)

Developing links with the Aboriginal community also allows the community to become involved with the provision of appropriate services to Aboriginal people. This can be of great assistance to mainstream services. In one example given, older women provided assistance in dealing with young "offenders":

> *The older women were particularly helpful in the establishment of boundaries... they would reprimand the young people, tell them not to speak disrespectfully to the workers, not to swear! And the young people usually responded really well to such discipline from their 'aunties'. There's no way they would have taken that from us non-Aboriginal workers ... The aunties provided the authority that we would struggle with ... There are still strong kinship ties between the families, kids respond to that.* (non-Aboriginal counsellor in an Aboriginal agency)

Within mainstream agencies, there should be a firm code of conduct that requires non-Aboriginal workers to be guided by their Aboriginal colleagues in matters affecting Aboriginal people.

Where independent Aboriginal services have been established to deal with particular issues, there needs to be a strong commitment, enshrined in legislation, for mainstream services:

- to consult with them on all matters concerning their area of responsibility.
- to follow the advice given in this consultation process.

> *Currently the Aboriginal Placement Principle is a recommendation that an Aboriginal child in need of a foster placement, should remain primarily in their biological family, within their extended family networks, or failing that, within the Aboriginal community.*
>
> *Aboriginal agencies expect mainstream agencies to follow this principle, but this often does not happen. Until the Aboriginal Placement Principle becomes enshrined in legislation, accountability still lies with mainstream agencies who are ultimately responsible for placement decisions. These decisions have been described as a reflection of subjective individual decisions, based on the whim of the individual worker. Legislation currently requires courts and mainstream services to contact the Aboriginal Child Care Agency, they are not obligated to*

take the placements we have to offer. We are still waiting for federal legislation to enshrine the Aboriginal Placement Principle in standard laws. There are a number of agencies which do not communicate with the Aboriginal Child Care Agency, and do not see it as the authorised agency to place Aboriginal children with. It's still left to the individual social worker to contact the agency. (Group interview with several welfare workers in an Aboriginal agency)

During interviews several examples of areas where consultation is particularly important were given. These included:

Following an admission of an Aboriginal person into a psychiatric institution, relevant members of the Aboriginal community should be contacted as soon as possible, so that they can meet the person admitted to determine whether the behaviour being displayed is, in fact, culturally acceptable. For example, in some circumstances, the hearing of voices by an Aboriginal person is deemed to be "normal". They are regarded as the voices of the spirit world. In other circumstances, voices are regarded as "abnormal", and non-Aboriginal mental health intervention is regarded as necessary. Consultation and involvement of Aboriginal people is the only way to find out what is appropriate, and even when western practices are deemed necessary, ongoing consultation is still necessary.

When Aboriginal people are admitted to any hospital, it is important that staff notify the Aboriginal Liaison Officers and seek their guidance and direction in dealing with the patient. Appropriate practices which may not immediately occur to non-Aboriginal Staff include having gender appropriate delivery of service:

- providing women nurses and doctors for women patients.
- *When a traditional man comes into hospital, and there are no Aboriginal male staff, it is more appropriate for him to be seen by a non-Aboriginal man than an Aboriginal woman staff member. However, consultation with the Aboriginal community remains of prime importance.* (Aboriginal community health nurse)

Accountability

During the interviews it was made clear that effective consultation depends on mainstream services gaining a different understanding of the concept of accountability. In this new understanding there needs to be:

- an open acknowledgement of the continuing history of injustice and oppression experienced by Aboriginal people.
- recognition that, in any attempt to address injustice, the group which has been responsible for perpetrating that injustice should be accountable to those who have experienced it.
- recognition that good intentions are not enough. Even when genuinely trying to "do the right thing" members of a dominant group are not always able to recognise when their own cultural perspective is involving them in practices that are unjust or oppressive.
- recognition that the best judges of whether an injustice has occurred are those people who have historically experienced injustice - not members of the dominant group.
- real power within the decision-making process needs to be invested with the Aboriginal people being consulted, rather than the dominant group continuing to have the ultimate say.

Mainstream agencies need to put structures in place that reflect these understandings of accountability, if their attempts at consultation are not to be seen as tokenistic.

Eduction and Training for Aboriginal People

Many people interviewed stressed the need for a wider availability of training and education in a variety of areas:

- Professional skills, such as counselling, nursing and medicine. The availability of this training would mean that Aboriginal staff could eventually replace non-Aboriginal staff in these sorts of positions.

  We need to train Aboriginal workers, particularly with the idea of encouraging them to gain skills that they could then go and provide services in culturally-appropriate ways through their own agencies. (non-Aboriginal health worker)

- How to operate effectively and survive within mainstream agencies.

Aboriginal people are not big talkers, but white people talk lots ... all the time. I felt a need to 'get training' so that I could maintain a job in a mainstream agency. I went to public speaking classes. It terrified me, but I learnt lots. I'm not afraid to speak up these days ... I used to be. (Aboriginal health worker)

- Knowledge of Aboriginal culture and history.

What about our history? ... I'd like, before I learn about anybody else's history, I'd really like to learn about my own ... I'm just finding out bits and pieces about it ... and it just makes me proud... makes me real proud. (Aboriginal health worker)

Aboriginal people should revisit their culture and bring back the aspects that make it work for us. (Aboriginal police aide)

Employment of Aboriginal staff

Having Aboriginal people in the waiting room at the office, so that when you walked in the door, there was an Aboriginal face to greet you ... It would be great to have Aboriginal staff, receptionists, doctors, nurses, community workers. (Aboriginal health care worker)

People interviewed stressed that the preference for self-determining and autonomous Aboriginal services does not absolve mainstream services from their responsibility to employ Aboriginal staff. The general presence of Aboriginal staff in both government and private organisations is necessary if Aboriginal people are to feel that they can access the services these organisations provide.

Aboriginal people generally do not have the same educational and employment opportunities as other groups in society. The following points concerning Aboriginal employment were made during interviews.

Aboriginal people want:

- permanency in employment so that when people do have jobs, they extend beyond 3 or 6 months.
- that there be career structures set in place, with vertical and horizontal mobility, so that people have opportunities to learn and to advance.
- that their Aboriginal skills and qualifications be recognised. While they may not have professional degrees, their experiences, understanding and knowledges are as valuable and should be recognised.
- that there be on-the-job training so that Aboriginal people can improve their formal qualifications.
- that their classifications be reviewed over time so that they can enjoy the same career and financial rewards as other groups in society.
- that they have autonomy over areas that specifically pertain to Aboriginal people - for example, Aboriginal community nurses conducting pap smears for Aboriginal women.
- that their expertise be utilised within their agency and that they direct their non-Aboriginal associates in issues concerning Aboriginal people.

Many people interviewed stressed that, if there is to be true "equal opportunity" for Aboriginal people, employers must engage in "affirmative action", in order to offset the existing environment of injustice and inequality. Among the services that were visited, a number were employing affirmative action strategies as listed below. They emphasised that any such strategies should be developed in consultation with Aboriginal people.

- cross-cultural awareness programmes for all members of staff.
- educating staff about the unique problems that beset Aboriginal people that may affect their ability to maintain their employment, e.g. high prevalence of morbidity and mortality.
- recognition that it is the responsibility of non-Aboriginal staff to educate themselves, especially about their own racism - it is not the responsibility of the Aboriginal staff to do so.
- employment of Aboriginal Liaison Officers to enable close networking between Aboriginal employees.

- not employing Aboriginal people in isolation; employing people from the same extended family, in order to utilise existing support structures. This also actively supports the Aboriginal values of caring and sharing, by providing the possibility for sharing employment opportunities with kin.
- Aboriginal staff placement - acting on the advice of Aboriginal employees regarding workplace location, taking into account aspects of access, transport and family commitments.
- recognition of Ceremonial needs, including special leave for attending funerals, in recognition of the high mortality rate among Aboriginal people, and the special role of funerals in their community life.
- recognition that, as Aboriginal people in South Austrlia constitute 1.5% of the population, then at least that same percentage of their workforce should be Aboriginal.

Non-Aboriginal people need to learn about and respect Aboriginal ways, knowledges, and meanings

Both Aboriginal and non-Aboriginal people interviewed stressed the need for non-Aboriginal people to inform themselves of, and show respect for, Aboriginal culture, and to recognise that Aboriginal people come from diverse groups, each with their own language, culture and practices. This diversity needs to be understood and respected.

> *Teach everyone about Aboriginal history, what's happened to them over the last 200 years, and how they've survived.* (Aboriginal director of an Aboriginal community centre)

This is not as an alternative to consultation, but to make effective consultation possible. Unless mainstream society develops such knowledge, understanding and respect, it cannot realistically enter into any a genuine relationship with the Aboriginal community.

Cultural education of non-Aboriginal staff in mainstream services was seen as particularly important, as they can have a major impact on Aboriginal people's lives without realising it.

> *A lot of our alcoholics don't take anything to hospital. Sometimes when they come into hospital, they might wet themselves, and we've actually had the situation where the nursing staff have rung up and said that they were going*

to burn their clothes. And we say, "don't you dare". We can put their clothes into a bag and take them back to their families to wash them. They don't have much, but the little bit they do have, they value. So it's in families like this that nursing staff need some education. This is where cultural awareness is so important. (Aboriginal health worker)

Non-Aboriginal staff also need to learn that the skills they have developed in dealing with people may not be at all relevant to Aboriginal people. Things that may have quite different meanings include:

- eye contact or the lack of it.
- body language generally.
- silence - it could mean a number of things including refusal, agreement, lack of understanding, or shame.
- ways of speaking - Aboriginal people are often perceived as speaking in tentative ways, however they are usually certain about what they want.

Non-Aboriginal staff also need to learn about behaviour of their own that could be disrespectful or shaming. This includes the need to be aware of appropriate language and not use terms such as "half-caste", "full-blood", "lubra" or "tribe".

We've often had concerns from the hospital about why is an Aboriginal person acting in a strange manner. So we go over there. We are planning some in-service on cultural awareness over at the nurse's station. But mainly it's going over and explaining. I can be an advocate for a patient, explain to the staff how this person feels, try and find out where the staff are coming from and explain how the client feels back. (Aboriginal health worker)

A preparedness to learn about and be open to different meanings are essential to an effective consultation process.

Examples given of areas where respect for Aboriginal ways is particularly needed included:

- Aboriginal people's need and duty to attend ceremonies and funerals. This requires special leave provisions for Aboriginal employees.

The Aboriginal community is a fluctuating community. They have strong family groups throughout the State and there are strong family commitments to return and visit relatives at certain times, especially if there is a funeral. (non-Aboriginal doctor at a community centre)

- Respect for the contribution of traditional Aboriginal healers and healing practices.

  Two-way medicine - it's a blend of traditional and conventional medicines, and it's being used on the Homelands more and more and it could be used in the hospitals. That would make the traditional people feel a bit more comfortable. (Aboriginal liaison officer)

Health Services should have a social focus, not a sickness focus

The most important elements of an ideal service would be that it reflects that health has a social focus rather than a sickness focus. This would mean that it's situated within a community that has a high Aboriginal population. It addresses holistic health needs. There'd be a vegie garden, and health workers would respect and believe traditional meanings of illness. There'd be outside space where people could meet and talk. Alternative cultural practices would be used. It should encompass all areas that contribute to health - like having food co-ops, housing officers that work there in the community. It would be owned and staffed by indigenous people. (non-Aboriginal community health nurse)

The physical layout of buildings in which services are provided, needs to be made more appropriate to Aboriginal ways

Suggestions made during the interviews included:

- Aboriginal posters; Aboriginal colours in the decor and furnishings.
- easy access to the outside to be able to sit with families, have a smoke, be able to laugh and talk without feeling that you are interrupting others.
- having an outside area where people can sit comfortably with appropriate seating, shelter, shade, lawn area.
- avoid long corridors and several sets of doors to have to walk through.
- in the waiting room have seats side-by-side, rather than opposite each

other. Have pamphlets and articles about Aboriginal activities and resources available.

• if there's a video available, have films about Aboriginal issues and culture as well as mainstream films.

We have a coffee room with a T.V. and a video, all videos on Aboriginal affairs throughout Australia. You know, like watching one video and then commenting on it, all sitting around and yarn about it later, over a coffee and that. A lot of Nungas are interested in what others are doing ... bands, storytelling, artists,.. you know, everything. (Aboriginal heath worker)

I wish we could joke ... Wish they had a room at the hospital where visitors could laugh, where you're not disturbing other patients. It really cheers the patient up. (Aboriginal health worker)

It would be nice to have an outside area where we could sit, have a joke, let the kiddies play, bait the dog. (Aboriginal health worker)

The organisation of services needs to be responsive to Aboriginal ways

The following points, relating to the way in which services are organised, were made during interviews:

• Aboriginal people want to establish a rapport with the person they are seeing, and this takes time.

• often Aboriginal people present to agencies with complex problems that cannot be addressed in the usual appointment times. What may be thought of as a simple case of 'thrush', for example, may in fact be a side-effect of diabetes.

• sometimes Aboriginal people, especially men, will not seek help until they are in crisis, requiring immediate attention.

• access and transport can be problematic for Aboriginal people, so people need to use the service when they are in the area. It's not always easy to "come back tomorrow".

- Aboriginal people may prefer to sleep on the floor and should have this choice.
- Lots of visitors should be allowed.

This place is not only for one person with a drug or alcohol problem but the whole family goes through a rehabilitation process. It's no good one person coming here and then going back home, [because] the families are then not used to that person; they are like strangers when they go back. But by being together, they can grow together. And there is no time-limit on how long anybody can stay here. (non-Aboriginal field worker at an Aboriginal service)

The decoration of the building reflects Aboriginal culture and it is regarded as Aboriginal land. The whole place is viewed as a safe place to go. The consultation stages are longer, and people can just walk in off the street, they don't have to make appointments, it's a 'first in - best dressed' situation, and everyone accepts that. While they are waiting to see the doctor, or whoever, they can attend cooking classes that are run there everyday, join the lunch, have a yarn. The doctor sits down to lunch everyday with everyone who is there. Children are encouraged to come, as are whole families. What is important for any people working with Aboriginal people, whether it be issues of health, or of a social nature, whatever, is that they must recognise that Aboriginal people operate under a different time-frame. You need to spend time with an Aboriginal client, time to get to know them and they you. Your first visit may be just to have a cup of tea and a social chat, the following visit is where you then begin to address the issues that have brought you there, ill-health, whatever. It's best not to speak about the problem immediately. They have been conducting a nutritional programme with the community and as a part of that, they have been planting fruit trees and vegetables at the centre. The community can come and reap the rewards. The vegies are used for lunches and as part of the nutrition programme. We now have a joint progamme being run in conjunction with other mainstream services. They provide us with a health nurse. They come to us, and through sharing of expertise and knowledges, are able to deal with complicated issues. They train Aboriginal workers, and are in time, guided by Aboriginal understandings. They take their direction from the Aboriginal people, the workers and the clients. (non-Aboriginal health worker at an Aboriginal community centre)

Issues of access need to be addressed

Aboriginal people often experience difficulty in accessing services due to poverty, lack of private or public transport, and remote location. Recommendations concerning how to address these issues included:

- Providing transport to assist Aboriginal people to attend appointments. Some agencies interviewed borrow the local community health centre's mini-bus. Taxi-vouchers are sometimes provided in cases of need.
- people from the Homelands visiting Adelaide for health reasons require special assistance with transport as often they are unfamiliar with public transport systems and with the lay-out of the city itself.
- outreach services prove successful in reaching Aboriginal people whom otherwise may not/cannot attend agencies.
- attending people in their own homes, or in their community, e.g. Aboriginal community centre, or the 'Nunga rooms' located in some of the primary schools; "going into their territory" rather than them having always to come to non-Aboriginal areas and services.

Specific recommendations made by Aboriginal people included:

A mini-bus would be good to get old people, women with kids to and from appointments, bring them into the centres ... help to take people to and from funerals. (Aboriginal community worker)

Another car and a mobile phone, that means we could be out in the community more, be more available in an emergency. (Aboriginal liaison officer)

Take dialysis machines to the community centres. People have to come here, sometimes for months on end, away from their families and their lands. It's very distressing for them. Much better if they could have the machines closer to home. (Aboriginal liaison officer)

We need community centres, or a drop-in centre. We need to have a place that's ours, where we can keep its touch, that's easy to get to near the shops, the bank. We need a place of our own. (Aboriginal community worker)

Acknowledgements

Aboriginal people:
Joe Agius, Tim Agius, Yvonne Agius, Cheryl Axelby, Jenny Baker, Chris Bonney, Brian Butler, Dave Cooper, Brian Dixon, John Dunn, Trevor Graham, Neville Gollan, Rosie Howsen, Pat Kartinyeri, Kath Lee, Jane Lester, Bronwyn McKenzie, Sandy Miller, Russell Milera, Sarah Milera, Peter Mitchell, Major (Moogie) Sumner, Sonny Morey, Lewis O'Brien, Tim O'Laughlin, Donna Popadopoulis, Colleen Prideaux, Leah Rankine, Rebeeca Tonkin, Frank Wanganeen, Rosemary Wanganeen, Janice Weetra, Rostind Weetra, Barbara Wingard, Sharon Wingard, Christine Urbanowski, Maureen Williams, Coral Wilson.

Non-Aboriginal people:
Rose Abbott, Steve Alsop, Jim Brunner, Alistair Bush, Jim Cane, Maggie Carey, Manuel Corral, Laz Cotsios, Brenda Crane, David Denborough, Matt Doherty, Jim Dunk, Kym Dwyer, John Gaites, Brian Gillan, Jenness Habel, Rob Hall, Gavin Hart, Tricia Hart, Catherine Hempell, Belinda Hermann, Alan Jenkins, Diana Jolly, Jon Jureidini, Anne Kasprzak, Christine Kingston, Frank Kinnear, Paula Lagnado, Peter Lake, Judy McDonald, Alan March, Veronica Mifsud, Helen Monten, Jim Mulvill, Rhonda Murray, Shalini Nambiar, Alison Newton, Mark Nugent, Ken O'Brien, Lindsay Osborn, Sally Pascoe, Gerry Patterson, Kym Peterson, Mick Piotto, Lesley Porter, Bruce Rankin, Lods Renney, Trevor Richardson, Judy Rumball, Lesley Shorne, Julie Silvers, Marie Steiner, Meg Strawbridge, David Sweet, Ray Tickner, Laurel Walker, Mark Waters, David Watts, Monica Winter. Christopher McLean for interviewing the members of the project team and then writing this report. Jussey Harbord and Carolyn Markey for planning and co-ordinating this research project.

The Aboriginal Health Council and Dulwich Centre wish to thank and acknowledge all those other people who made a contribution to this research.

Note

1. This chapter was previously published in Aboriginal Health Council of South Australia, 1995: 'Reclaiming Our Stories, Reclaiming Our Lives', *Dulwich Centre Newsletter*, No.1

13

Working together

By

Barb Wingard and Michael Bentley

'If we're working together, we can get to know each other.'

This chapter explores working relationships within the Hills Mallee Southern Region of South Australia in which I am the Aboriginal Health Services Co-ordinator. The following pages include extracts from a report that was written in June 2000 by myself and Michael Bentley who is the Principal Planning and Research Officer in the Hills Mallee Southern Regional Health Service.

Background

The Hills Mallee Southern Region is one of seven country health regions of South Australia which were created five years ago with the aim of improving planning and delivery of health services. The region comprises of diverse geographical areas along the Murray River, the Mallee, the Adelaide Hills, the Fleurieu Peninsula and Kangaroo Island and has an estimated population of 120,000 people of whom about 1400 (as counted at the 1996 census) are Aboriginal.

The region extends over the land of three different Aboriginal peoples. The Ngarrindjeri people are the traditional owners of the land that forms a significant part of the Hills Mallee Southern Region. Ngarrindjeri land extends from Swanreach on the Murray river, down to Kingston in the South East, and west to Cape Jarvis on the Fleurieu Peninsula. The Peramangk people are the traditional owners of the Adelaide Hills. And the Adelaide Plains (on the western side of the Hills Mallee Southern Region) are the traditional lands of the Kaurna people.

In 1995, when the country heath services in South Australia were placed into regions, regional health service boards were established to oversee local and regional service provision. The Hills Mallee Southern Regional Board draws its membership from local health service boards with additional places for Aboriginal and consumer groups and for members of the medical profession. There are also expert nominees with financial, legal and management skills.

The initial Aboriginal representative on the Hills Mallee Southern Regional Board was Shirley Gollan. A number of us felt that it would be important to find some way of supporting her and to introduce other board members to the issues of Aboriginal health in the region. We took a number of steps which are described here by the Hon. M.H. Armitage in his Report in the House of Assembly – Estimates Committee (27th June 1996):

'The members of the Hills Mallee Southern Regional Board were recently involved in the development of initiatives to support the Aboriginal representative on the board, Shirley Gollan. The Aboriginal Health Worker and the regional CEO (respectively Barbara Wingard and Kevin Eglinton) organised a cultural awareness day for board members. They involved local Aboriginal people from Camp Coorong, Point McLeay [Raukkan], Tailem Bend, Murray Bridge and Kalparrin. The local board members were taught about the history of Aboriginal health in the area, the health services that Aboriginal people need, how they could be provided, how to ensure that they were accessible to Aboriginal people and so on. They discussed how future consultation should occur with the Aboriginal people in the area and how to support the single Aboriginal representative on the board.*

It was there that the decision was made that a regional Aboriginal advisory group should be formed which would have two nominated representatives from each of the areas that I mentioned The role of that advisory group will be to provide relevant information, support, advice and so on to the Aboriginal representative on the regional board. ... I have to say that this is a fantastic initiative from the Aboriginal community because sometimes the machinations of the board decisions might well seem irrelevant to some members of the Aboriginal community and it is very important that the Aboriginal representative on the board is supported. I am very pleased with that outcome.'

Researching working relations

Following the introduction of regionalisation in country South Australia and this early acknowledgement of Aboriginal Health issues on the regional board, it seemed timely in the Year 2000 to document the progress of Aboriginal Health Services in the Hills Mallee Southern region. We wanted to gather together stories from Aboriginal people and non–Aboriginal people who are involved in the deliver of services and also those who are managing services. To do so we held 28 interviews with Aboriginal health workers, non-Aboriginal workers (managers, colleagues and/ or mentors), Aboriginal health service board members at regional and local board levels, and non-Aboriginal health service board members (nominees and ex-officio members).

What we found:

Those who we interviewed spoke about a number of significant changes that have occurred in relation to Aboriginal Health in the Hills Mallee Southern Region over the last five years.

More Aboriginal Health Workers

Firstly, there are more Aboriginal Health Workers in place and this has according to those we interviewed, had significant effects:

- *'I never saw an Aboriginal face in this service till [the Aboriginal Health Workers] came'* (non-Aboriginal health worker)
- *'There was not one client before. Now we have 15 registered clients'* (Aboriginal health worker)

Improved training

Many of the Aboriginal Health Workers are currently studying for, or have completed primary health care certificates as well as diabetes educator's courses.

- *'Now that training has been identified, we are trained and identified as professionals in our own right.'* (Aboriginal health worker)

- *'The quality, diversity and volume of training for Aboriginal Health Workers have greatly increased over the last ten years. They are not just door openers or band-aids. They negotiate better access and quality for their clients.'* (Aboriginal Board Member)

Improved communication and co-operation

- *'It's going along really well at the moment. There has been a huge effort in communication and co-operative ideas.'* (non-Aboriginal health worker)

- *'[It's been important to] build up the relationships and network with outside services.'* (Aboriginal health worker)

An increased emphasis on a primary health care approach

- *'It comes down to being able to be more proactive in primary health care – taking programs to the community.'* (Aboriginal health worker)

Better planning

- *'The fact that [the Aboriginal health worker] is permanent means that they can plan for the longer term.'* (non-Aboriginal health worker)

Better services

- *'Just having [an Aboriginal Health Worker] around has been important. They know the community and provide the link and the culture.'* (non- Aboriginal health worker)

- *'The key is people being responsible for their own health and their children. The credit goes back to the community for taking the ownership.'*
  (Aboriginal health worker)

- *'The Aboriginal Health Workers plan well together, for example, in addressing family ties and the strong link with the needs of a child in hospital.'* (non-Aboriginal health worker)

Support for Workers

A number of factors have proved to be important in supporting Aboriginal Health Workers. The first was the establishment of an Aboriginal Health Workers' Network. This is seen as possibly the most important support mechanism in the region. The network was established in 1996 and has grown and strengthened:

- *'I value the Health Worker meetings. I learn from that and get the help and support and the resources. I can ring the other health workers and get a lot of ideas and support where others have tried things out.'*
- *'We're there to support each other and to lean on each other'*
- *'Relationships with other Aboriginal health workers are important – it's great that there are different styles, ages and gender differences. We learn to work in harmony together.'*

Another significant development has been the introduction of mentors for new workers. Mentoring is a relationship in which one person supports another to develop their knowledges and skills. Mentoring can be both formal and informal. Both ways are currently being used in the region. This is working well:

'In terms of organisation, the new worker is responsible to me – we have that close link. It is easier for them to catch up with me and we are able to solve the issues together.' (non-Aboriginal Health Worker)

Support for Aboriginal members on Board of Directors

Aboriginal people are now on the boards of directors of various health services and hospitals in the Hills Mallee Southern Region. This is very positive development and the Aboriginal members on health boards are supported in the collegiate sense in that the boards provide the same level of support to Aboriginal members as any other member.

- *'I'm not just there as a token.'* (Aboriginal board member)
- *'Originally members thought I was just there for the Aboriginal issues but now they realise I am there for the big picture.'* (Aboriginal board member)
- *'I help [the Aboriginal member] feel comfortable. If they weren't comfortable they wouldn't attend.'* (non-Aboriginal board member)
- *'The Aboriginal member brings an Aboriginal perspective and cultural difference to an otherwise all-white Board.'* (non-Aboriginal board member)

Despite this collegiate support, it is still possible for Aboriginal Board members to experience cultural isolation in their role. Aboriginal people consist of a diverse group of communities. A single member on a board sits in isolation, which can present problems both in terms of support in meetings and also in terms of reporting back to Aboriginal communities. One strategy around this is to allow a second Aboriginal person to sit on the board as an observer, a proxy member or as a non-voting member.

- *"Two members could give each other support. Is it a special case or does it mean that everyone else would have one?'* (non-Aboriginal Board Member)
- *'A significant barrier is that all people see themselves as nominees representing their community. They can't see the difficulty for Aboriginal people to reflect themselves in a Western system. Two members would allow support. The others have support – they are all European.'* (non-Aboriginal Board Member)

What does 'culturally appropriate' mean?

A key aspect of the research was to ask workers and board members about their understandings of what 'culturally appropriate' means. In this section we have recorded the different themes that came up from our conversations with Aboriginal Health Workers and non-Aboriginal Health Workers.

When asked about their understandings of 'cultural appropriateness', Aboriginal Health Workers spoke of three themes: *respect, understanding* and *inclusion.*

Respect: Aboriginal Workers spoke of the importance for non-aboriginal workers to respect their law, their dignity and their culture and beliefs. They also spoke about the need to acknowledge the history of the last 200 years.

Understanding: Aboriginal workers believed there were a number of areas that required understanding in order to act in culturally appropriate ways:

- understanding where people are coming from, their lives, their history

- understanding the importance of speaking in ways that people can understand, ie. no jargon

- understanding what suits people in minority groups in the community

- understanding how to act sensitively

Inclusion: Aboriginal workers spoke of the importance of inclusion, of ensuring there were no barriers that excluded people's access to services, and ensuring that there was no prejudice. They also spoke of the need for services to adapt to the hopes and dreams of the community.

When we asked non-Aboriginal workers about their understandings of the 'cultural appropriateness', they spoke of four themes: *respect, access, education* and *acceptance.*

Respect: Non-Aboriginal people spoke of the need to respect Aboriginal customs as well as their cultural values and morals. It was felt that it was important to try to understand what was important to people from their backgrounds.

Access: Workers spoke of the need to ensure that there were no cultural barriers that would stop people accessing services and that the only way to find this out was to consult with Aboriginal people.

Education: Non-Aboriginal Workers spoke of the need for non-Indigenous people to learn about the different issues facing Aboriginal people as well as about their cultural heritage.

Acceptance: Finally, non-Aboriginal workers spoke of their responsibility to ensure that Aboriginal people feel a level of comfort when they are accessing services so that they feel as if they belong there.

What would a culturally appropriate service look like?

We then asked Aboriginal and non-Aboriginal workers what they believed a culturally appropriate service would look like.

Aboriginal workers spoke of access, choice, comfort, training and consultation:

- *'A drop-in centre with easy access.'*
- *'A place where all Aboriginal members could come – although they might need one of us to be with them.'*
- *'There needs to be lots of choices, so that people can identify that they were being respected.'*
- *'A place of Aboriginal-specific information resources.'*
- *'A place where there are Aboriginal faces around to help people feel more comfortable.'*
- *'It's all about attitudes and the ways in which people are treated when they come in.'*
- *'Services need to be familiar with indigenous people and their cultures, through co-operative working relationships and specific / specialist cross-cultural awareness programs.'*
- *'Community consultation needs to take place in the process of developing a culturally appropriate service.'*

Non-Aboriginal workers spoke of community consultation, choice, access and flexibility:

- *'Our service would look very different. We would need to see that the service develops with Aboriginal people as part of the planning.'*
- *'I believe it's about a service being conducted where the community wants it to be.'*

- *'You would need to do a community consultation to meet the needs and find out what is appropriate, but it must be within the budget.'*
- *'A culturally appropriate service would be run by Aboriginal people'*
- *'Aboriginal women need a choice or option of a male or female worker. The women may not be comfortable when men are also coming to the service.'*
- *'A service that enables access to traditional knowledge, beliefs and practices.'*
- *'It would need to be flexible, diverse, non-conformist, consultative, reactive and proactive, accountable, responsive and inclusive of acute care as well as community health workers.'*
- *'We'd need a lot of cross cultural awareness and training.'*

Cross Cultural Awareness and Training

Throughout the interviews both Aboriginal and non-Aboriginal Health Workers spoke about the importance of cross cultural awareness training. Workers spoke about the difference that cultural awareness training does make.

- *'A good story was when a non-Aboriginal worker asked an Aboriginal Health Worker if she was a quarter Aboriginal, etc. The non-Aboriginal worker apologised after participating in awareness training'* (Aboriginal Health Worker)

There were a number of issues that workers felt were important to be covered in cultural awareness training:

- *'Describe events that took place in history.'*
- *'Define and understand how an Aboriginal family works.'*
- *'Break down myths and stereotypes.'*
- *'Teach people how to understand Aboriginal English.'*
- *'Inform workers about where Aboriginal people are coming from. Provide information so that workers can make informed decisions.'*
- *'Let people know about the policies and their effects on the Indigenous peoples*

of Australia-the ways in which people were excluded from mainstream services – health, welfare, employment, housing, voting rights.'

Most workers felt that this training was needed for all new workers and that it also needed to be ongoing. Aboriginal Health Workers said that they believed they ought to play an active role in organising this training but that they believed it was the responsibility of management to support this training and to ensure that it occurs.

- *'The mainstream organisation need to fully support training. Health workers could organise it but it needs to be supported by the management and made a priority.'* (Aboriginal Health Worker)

Non-Aboriginal workers spoke about how this training is everyone's responsibility, but again how management has a crucial role to play:

- *'There needs to be a partnership arrangement as employers and employees both have responsibilities in this area. Individuals have a responsibility to learn for themselves. If they are working in Aboriginal communities they should find out about them.'* (non-Aboriginal Health Worker)

Working relationships

Throughout the research, most Aboriginal Health Workers reported having developed good working relationships within mainstream services. We were interested in hearing about the steps that they have taken to work alongside other health professionals:

- *'I ask other workers to come with me on home visits.'*
- *'Being in the job a while helps. If I've supported them and worked in well the first time then they're quick to pick the phone up and do it again. My priority is to get in their early, to be pro-active.'*
- *'I try to build a lot of respect and trust. People ask me whether certain thing are an issue for Aboriginal people or not and we nut out what they don't*

understand about Aboriginal culture. If I don't know what they need to know
I go and find out the information.'

- 'I slowly get to know them and teach them which little things look offensive.'

- 'Just being me. I yarn. You are who you are. If you cannot accept yourself, you
can't expect others to accept you.'

- 'If I need advice I go up and ask. If they need help they ask me.'

What hinders Aboriginal Health Service development?

During the interviews a number of factors were identified as barriers or hindrances
to Aboriginal Health Service development. These included funding, a lack of choice
and mistaken beliefs:

Funding

- A lack of recurrent funding makes planning very difficult. Twelve-month time-
frames are too short.
- Funding Aboriginal Health Worker positions then leaving them to work in
isolation has not been successful.

Choice

- A lack of appropriate clinics for Aboriginal people.
- A lack of choice of male/female Aboriginal Health Workers.

Mistaken beliefs

People have many values and beliefs that they hold, some of which are offensive
and hurtful to Aboriginal people. These values and beliefs often come from a lack of
awareness, knowledge or experience. We have included here some quotes from
Aboriginal Health Workers about their struggles in dealing with other workers'
mistaken beliefs.'

- 'People have a lot of different values and beliefs. I have to speak to them about
culturally inappropriate treatment. Some could be more culturally aware.'

- *'A few comments that have been made by uneducated staff, staff who haven't had cultural awareness training, can be hurtful, eg: 'Aboriginal health gets everything', 'I could do your job', 'Is he half-Aboriginal?. These sorts of things fall into the myths and stereotypes about Aboriginal people.'*
- *'Some staff have made comments that are racist. If these comments are being said inside the service, then what is being said to people outside? What image is being filtered into the community by these workers?'*
- *'We have to look carefully at the columns of prejudice / racism in education and political systems. We have to address institutional racism.'*

Influencing the mainstream

All participants saw themselves as involved in addressing these barriers. When we asked Aboriginal Health Workers about their role in influencing the mainstream in relation to Aboriginal health, here are some of the things they said:

- *"We act as a cultural broker, a liaison on issues, and as advocacy agent. We also advocate for funding.'*
- *'If we're not there seeking changes and giving advice then the services may treat Aboriginal people inappropriately.'*
- *'We help the other workers understand Aboriginal culture, basic things like what they should do and what they shouldn't talk about.'*
- *'We try to bring the staff and Aboriginal people together.'*

We asked Non-Aboriginal Health Workers what role they saw non-Aboriginal managers having in influencing the mainstream about Aboriginal Health. Here are some of their responses:

- *'If you are responsible for a worker then it is a part of your role to be in there batting for them.'*
- *'It's my role to advocate for Aboriginal Health Workers to levels of management above me.'*
- *'Managers need to be looking at funding for ongoing resources, making sure that the service is ongoing and appropriate, and that training happens.'*

- *'We are the movers and shakers of the business plans. I support flexibility.'*
- *'We must keep up the cultural awareness training.'*
- *'Support, acknowledge and respect the Aboriginal Health Workers' role.'*
- *'Managers have a huge role. It's about where services are provided. For example, does a leafy-green suburb need the same presence as a socially disadvantaged area?'*
- *'Managers have a role to advocate for their client groups, to support practitioners in fulfilling their roles, and to be a leader and role model.'*
- *'Lobbying for influence at federal, state and local levels on programs.'*
- *'It only works if everyone has a role.'*

Overall themes that have emerged

From all the conversations we shared with Aboriginal and non-Aboriginal health workers, a number of key themes have emerged. We have tried to summarise them here.

- The presence of Aboriginal members on health boards has increased the awareness and understanding of Aboriginal issues within the region.

- Having Aboriginal Workers in mainstream services is providing a link to the community. Aboriginal people are using services - they don't always come to the mainstream service, the service often goes to them.

- It takes Aboriginal Health Workers time to build knowledge, relationships, confidence and trust. Twelve month contracts limit the ability to develop meaningful relationships. Being in the job for 2-3 years appears to help in developing good working relationships with other health professionals but this depends on the individual worker's skills and experiences.

- An effective Aboriginal Health Workers' Network can assist in the improvement of Aboriginal Health Services.

- The acknowledgement of the importance of Aboriginal Health Workers working in flexible ways needs constant support from management, particularly where mistaken beliefs may create tensions within the service.

- Various approaches to cultural awareness are needed. Cross-cultural training is seen as important but it needs to be ongoing. Visiting Aboriginal communities, whether in groups (as for Board members) or as individuals (as with non-Aboriginal workers accompanying Aboriginal Health Workers) can be more appropriate than formal training sessions in some cases.

- A holistic primary health care focus is not only important in Aboriginal Health but also necessary to the effective delivery of all health services. This is not just about outcomes - it's about the way we do things.

- The distribution of Aboriginal Health Workers across the region is uneven with a lack of choice in relation to female/male workers in some areas.

- Participants had clear understandings and ideas about what is culturally appropriate in health services. What culturally appropriate services would look like needs further Aboriginal community consultation. Issues of access and choice are important.

Last words

It seems appropriate to leave the last words to the Aboriginal Health Workers of the region:

- *'If you want equality then you don't treat people the same. Things need to be done differently.'*

- *'We're expected to do a lot by the community and we wouldn't be in these positions, or we wouldn't last long, if we didn't have the community at heart.'*

- *'I want to get out to help people; the paper work is the problem.'*

- *'We've made an effort to get out and talk to the community at their level.'*

- *'I would like a culturally appropriate place to work from. If I had a clinic, clients could just drop in when they like.'*

- *'If I didn't think I was making a difference, then I wouldn't be here. It's not for the money.'*

- *'It's not a job, it's a lifestyle. You're working with your own people.'*

- *'If we're working together, we can get to know each other.'*

Acknowledgements:

The participants for giving their time and energy to this project: Tony Barrett, Karen Bates, Sharon Bland, Rick Brandon, Joe Byrne, Marion Cheshire, Jenny Cooke, Ashley Couzens, Kevin Eglinton, Bonnie Fisher, Kathleen Gregurke, Barry Griffin, Andrea Henschke, Sandra Lawrie, Ailene Lawson, Kathryn Leslie, Elaine Mant, Michael Pengilly, Sharon Perkins, Darrell Sumner, Brian Taylor, fred Toogood, Elizabeth Warne, Bill Wilson, Di Wilson, Sandra Wilson, Audrey Windram.

We'd also like to acknowledge The Meningie, Murray Bridge and Strathalbyn Hospitals, the Murray Mallee Community Health and Southern Fleurie Health Services, the Raukkan community Council, Child and Youth health Services, The Mannum Community club, the Riverscape Café, Audrey Windram and Michael Pengilly for assisting in providing suitable environments for the interviews. Chris Caleiden for helpful comments on the draft report.

Note

This chapter has been adapted from the report 'Working Together:' published by Hills Mallee Southern Region Area Health, 2000.

14

Hopefulness and pride

by

Barbara Wingard

As we come to the end of this book it seems an important time to be looking towards the past and also towards the future. As Aboriginal people, these days it is more important than ever to be acknowledging our elderly. Some of our young ones do not have many elderly people in their lives. Our people do not live for as long as they should, and so a lot of our younger ones rely on us, people in our fifties, early sixties, to be their elders – to support them and acknowledge them, and to help create paths for them to find their way through. It is our place to be here for our young folk.

When I think of our elderly and when I think of our young ones, it brings a sense of pride. It is a pride that flows from the past to the present to the future. We Indigenous Australians are proud people. We may not have a lot of money, but we can maintain our culture and the pride that goes with this. We are very proud of who we are, what we do and how we achieve it. I believe that our old people were proud people. They stood tall, with their heads up. When you look within old photographs, the first thing you see is our old people's pride. Because of all that has happened in this country, when you look at more recent photographs sometimes you see a different look, a look of our people struggling to reclaim our lives, our culture and our dignity.

I often wonder what it is that has enabled us to keep alive our pride. In preparing these words I spoke with Karen Bates, who is twenty and is now working in the Aboriginal Health Worker Position which once I worked in. We sat by the Murray River one morning as she told me what she believed made people proud.

She said, 'A knowledge of who you are, where you come from, who your family is. It is about knowing what happened in the past, knowing what your family has been through. It is also about wanting to make people aware, to make a difference.'

This pride comes from a knowledge of hard times. It is a pride of knowing what we have been through, a pride of knowing our stories and finding ways of sharing them with others who want to hear. Pride is a lovely word.

It seems an important time to be looking towards the past and also towards the future. I have a very special feeling in my heart towards our young ones. They are our future. These young people will continue when I am not around. They will continue to offer their hearts and minds to others. They will continue to give to their communities. Knowing this brings hopefulness to me. Hopefulness and pride.